Charlotte,
Thank you for [illegible]
your assistance in my dental care!
You are an awesome woman!

A Woman with No Name

A Journey of Survival

Debra Jean

A Woman with No Name

A Journey of Survival

ISBN-13: 978-1503302051

ISBN-10: 1503302059

Cover Design by Damonza.com

DEDICATION

In loving memory of my mother, Bernadette

I miss you every single moment of my life-In God's Care.

ACKNOWLEDGEMENTS

To **Dr. Amy Wrabetz** who taught me how to honor, to love, and to forgive myself. Thank you for being my support system throughout the years, showing me tenderness and kindness, and your sincere devotion to my well-being. You have been an amazing advocate for me and for many veterans. You truly are an angel here on earth covering all of us with your massive wings of love.

To my **Lord**, my **God**, my **Savior**, for you have never left my side during the darkest days of my life and for continually loving me and showing me grace.

To all of my beloved dogs who carried me through this journey of survival, my family: **Alex**, **Bronte**, **Cosette**, and **RardoBoy**: the Jelly Bean Gang-forever in my heart as you wait under the rainbow bridge for me. My dogs gave me purpose, as I searched to enter into a life of dignity. They healed my deeply imbedded wounds from years of abuse by showing me unconditional love. And to my precious **Zena Marie**, my emotional support dog, thank you for continuing to heal me with your loving ways. You are my heart.

To my fellow **Veterans**, who served the United States of America with honor and sacrificed their lives for freedom-my deepest gratitude-thank you. And to those **Veterans** who suffer on the daily battlefield coping with PTSD, TBI, depression, and homelessness, may God keep granting each and every one of you the strength and the hope to carry the fight into the dawn of the next day, for you are my true Warriors.

To **Jeffrey Miller**, author—I am profoundly grateful and appreciative for your guidance, support, and assistance into the realm of self-publishing.

To **Wilbur**, for watching over my dogs, helping me move countless times, giving me shelter, and so much more-my sincere thank you.

To **Christopher Kosa Sakamaki**, for your forgiveness, and the countless conversations we had about human behavior - "the tribe has spoken."

To **Antoinette (Toni) Diddle**, for being my second mother.

To **Robin Callan-Chicago Robini**, for experiencing life's ups and downs and having the best times of our lives in Chi-Town.

To **Connie Haeseley**, for your consistent encouragement to publish my story.

To **Erica May Slavens**, for calling me *Momma*-so proud of you-all my love.

To **Debra Sue Kambury**, for your loyalty, love, and friendship.

To **Allen Boettcher**, forever in my heart-my marine.

To **Tim Gunderman**, for your true friendship and deep loyalty.

To **Rick Marzetta**, for all of your support, laughs, and friendship.

To all of my **Facebook Friends**, for supporting me and being my Internet family. I thank you for showing me encouragement and love.

For the Lamb at the center of the throne will be their shepherd; he will lead them to springs of living water. And God will wipe away every tear from their eyes.

Revelations 7-17 NIV

PROLOGUE

Naples, Italy 1984

A BLANKET OF peacefulness covered the indolent town of Pozzuoli, tucking in its people already deep in sleep to escape the warmth of the afternoon sun. I drove through the narrow filthy streets, which were surprisingly free of traffic. Stacked apartments lined both sides of the streets, as yesterday's laundry hung from balconies to dry in the salty breeze.

My Volkswagen puffed up the washed out road to the naval hospital. Upon my desperate ascent, I realized that at no time does one really know the depths of another's pain.

Earlier that morning, I received the heartbreaking news that my roommate, Anna, almost ended her life with the careless sweep of a razor's edge.

Shore Patrol tapped on the door of our barracks with no intention of waiting for a verbal response, as they entered with their two slobbering dogs of German descent: Adolph and Stalin. The canine unit sniffed through our lockers and located our food as questions about Anna attacked my sleepy head. My awakening eyes focused through the Sandman's remains and onto Anna's empty bed. Since that moment, my mind could not absorb the unknown events that took place in Anna's life within the past twenty-four hours.

***

Finally, my Volkswagen made it to the top of the hill where the naval hospital stood at attention. I drove upon the heat-laden blacktop and stopped between the designated stripes. The bottom of my thighs slid off the vinyl car seat leaving behind a smear of sweat. I walked across the parking lot and entered the hospital with hesitation.

Just like any other military installation, women and men in starchy white uniforms walked in unison throughout the hallways. The corpsman sitting behind the patient information desk told me that Anna was on the fourth floor, the psychiatric ward. I passed the ancient elevator and climbed the stairs. Reaching the fourth floor, I leaned against the emergency door to calm my breathing. Pressing my aching forehead against the coolness of the square glass embedded in the steel door, I pressed the intercom button. Gathering what military bearing I possessed, I entered a world of minds filled with mystery.

The lifeless halls glared from the abundance of artificial wax used to bring some sunshine to this place of gloom. The stench of urine and body odor drifted from the rooms as I passed by. Neither a careless breeze nor an oscillating fan moved the stagnant air that consumed the nauseating hallway.

I was afraid to turn my head and look inside the room, but curiosity forced my eyeballs to stretch until they reached the corners of my eyes. I only caught a glimpse of a bony leg, as the faceless owner screamed that she did not want to eat her apple.

At last, I approached Anna's room and tiptoed inside. Her sutured wrists and ankles were bound by leather restraints. Sweat pasted her hair alongside her neck and forehead. The insides of her thighs appeared to be coated with a pimply rash, as she laid in her own excretions that saturated the sheets. The opened back gown was her only attire.

Anna's body was motionless except for her diaphragm. It rose hesitantly, lightly confirming that life still harbored inside of her. My knees hit the title floor as if someone had swung a wooden bat into the back of my legs.

Anna parted her cracked lips to speak to me, but her hidden voice could not be found. A thin line of drool seeped from her gaping mouth as a tear slid down the side her face. Feeble attempts were made to struggle out of her clenching leather restraints, but Anna's attempts lost against the powerful medication that infected her brain. Her usual dancing, black irises, and passionate, emerald eyes were replaced with enlarged pupils, enticing me down into a current of darkness that captured Anna's soul.

I laid my shaking body next to the stillness of hers. Placing my tear stained face in the nape of her neck, I held her close until the sun exchanged places with the moon.

My name is Debra Jean, and I am Anna. This is my story.

CHAPTER ONE

SOME DAYS, I don't know how my bloody footprints walked with my weakened steps among the dusty road of life to travel in the storms of sand. My sole possessions packed in a blanket of woven dreams that had frayed; I take one more step each day upon the earth. Memories that never leave my mind present themselves each morning, as I lie in bed staring at the ceiling knowing it would be much easier to keep my mother's quilt wrapped tightly around me, to keep life out, and her scent in. I do not want my foot to touch the cold floor.

Life, I don't want to face you today.

How do I lift my wary arm and knock on the door of rejection one more time? Picking up a piece of glass or a razor blade and pressing the sharpness of those co-dependent friends into the softness of my skin is a choice I face when stress overtakes my life.

I am a cutter; I self-mutilate. This label became attached to me after moments in time when the appearance of pride no longer showed its face, and the poise of grace no longer bowed.

Why do the powerful turn to the beggars to feast? A question that remains unanswered to me.

I want to go back in time and change the outcome of those tortuous events that lasted ninety-six hours in 1984 in Naples, Italy that changed me forever. Ninety-six hours. How I wished I had never walked through that doorway. The doorway where I met evil and evil descended upon me and crushed the existence of my spirit and body leaving my heart bloodless for all eternity.

When my eyes awake to greet the day and close at night to relive the horrors in the darkness of my dreams, I regret walking through that door. The wells of my memory carry the atrocities every day, as I shuffle through life looking for my heart to be filled with a richness of new blood: a new memory.

However, my story does not begin in 1984. It began when I was eight years old while standing at the side of my mother's hospital bed. As I stood there afraid to touch her, grape jelly stains covered my t-shirt and matted hair stuck to my scalp.

She did not look like my mother; she looked like Frankenstein. Green stitches wrapped around her neck along with purple X's that were splashed all over her chest. The X's marked the spots where the mega doses of radiation zapped and burned away her cancer.

She began to cry.

I had to take care of myself.

My mother's thyroid and parathyroid gland were removed because she found a lump one day while looking in the mirror. It was cancerous. She was thirty-one years old, and everything changed for her and our family. Nothing was ever going to be the same again.

The sun still rose in the east, and the moon appeared on the night's black canvas, but the normal world turned into a lost world without the sun, as darkness hovered all around me.

Every day after school, my sister, Janie and I went across the street to the Fenn's house until our father or grandmother came and got us. We stayed in their basement and played with puzzles, a fake grocery store, and of course, the TV set was always on. TV became my escape and best friend while growing up, as it still is today.

We accessed the house through the garage door and immediately went to the basement. I felt less than the other two children that lived there because I could not play in their rooms, the living room, or even use the upstairs bathroom.

One day I snuck into the girl's bedroom. I walked into a room of a fairy princess. The scent of lavender filled the air, as it lingered on my clothes. I was fascinated with the lacey pink bedspread and sliver plated handle of her hand-held mirror.

What caught my eye more than anything else in the room was a candle shaped like an old-fashioned soda fountain glass. The silver cup looked like the ones at Frank's Cigar and Ice Cream Store in our nearby town. Sitting on her dresser, the candle formed two scoops of chocolate ice cream, had a cherry on top, and a real straw sticking out of it. I bent down and placed my nose at the tip of the candle to smell its sweetness. Then, I ran out of the bedroom, opened up the garage door, and hurried across the street.

My sister and I were the orphans with the sick mother in the neighborhood.

But thankfully, the Fenns took us in, which they were paid by my mother, until the time came for our family to move.

My family lived in a brand new ranch style house at 2410 13th Street in Peru, Illinois; the home was on the west end of town. We lived there for five years. At eight years of age, I begged my parents for a new purple bedroom. Finally, I got it.

Within that same year, I had to leave that bedroom behind. It was the one thing that was all mine until the cancer took my house away. Moving to the east side of town was our only option. But more importantly, cancer was taking my mother away.

***

Janie and I had to share a room in our new, tiny white house with red shutters. There were only two bedrooms and one bathroom in the house we moved into on Prospect Street. We could lie in our beds and touch hands. It was like living in a closet. I missed my purple bedroom, the only home I could remember, friends, and our big backyard. Living in this tiny house, going to a new school, and meeting new friends were not on my agenda. Especially the closet bedroom. I wanted my old life back and to see my mother standing by the kitchen sink wearing her pale, blue housecoat while making silver dollar pancakes. She never entered by life again on any emotional or a physical level like it was before the cancer, even though she survived it this time.

CHAPTER TWO

THE UNIVERSITY OF Iowa City Hospital and Clinics and Powers Motel became our permanent residencies. After Ma had surgery, she continually had to go back to the hospital in Iowa City for body scans that took six to eight hours. They started at the top of her head and went all the way down to her toes. She had to remain perfectly still for the technicians to record an accurate report. The pressure of the hospital, food, motel, and fuel bills and driving back and forth to Iowa City with two kids in the back seat of the car was overpowering for anyone. As we struggled financially, emotionally, spiritually, and physically, we didn't dare speak of the turbulence disrupting the our household.

The beatings began because life changed so drastically for us. Stress will always find a way out. And usually, stress will always find its way out of the body. It disguises itself in behaviors that emerge into ugliness.

After one of our many trips back from Iowa City, our family stopped outside the National Dry Cleaners on Peoria Street. My parents, especially Ma, had to be exhausted from the drive and the scans.

Mentally worn down, my mother got out of the car, walked into the cleaners, and picked up a jacket while Dad smoked his Victory cigarette in the front seat of our golden Impala.

Janie and I loved reading *MAD* magazines or any nonsensical reading material to keep our minds engaged in fiction instead of the reality of our lives. As usual, I was goofing off and tried to imitate the cover of the magazine. The caricature held his arms up like he just became the champion of a sporting event. His exaggerated hairy armpits popped out as he raised his arms over his head in celebration. Imitating the cover, I clenched my hands together and shook them like I was the champion. Forgetting I had a blue pen in my hand, I drew a mark on the inside of the car's roof. Trying to make my sister laugh did not go as I had planned.

The mark did not seem to go unnoticed. My father's eagle eyes caught the mistake as deadly silence filled the car. His massive hands with knuckles the size of walnuts grabbed me by my collar. He hoisted me from the back seat and into the front. Then he punched me in my arm and shook me until my teeth mashed together.

As Ma got back inside the car with a hand full of dry cleaned laundry, she began to yell at me.

***

About a year later, my sister, father, and I were driving to Rockford. Janie saw a dermatologist. These treatments were really painful for her.

I took her sadness inside with me. Making her laugh for just one moment was a mission I set out to do, so she could forget about her situation.

There was a sign I saw on the side of the road that read "AVIS." I made a jingle with the name "DAVIS." Sitting in the middle between my sister and father in the front seat, I repeated the jingle until my father exploded. He jabbed his elbow like a sword into my ribs. All the air in my lungs gushed out. I thought my ribs were broken. In pain, I choked back the tears, and sat there silently. Janie looked out the passenger's side window.

I got beat for everything: laughing, goofing off, not doing something the right way like washing the dishes properly, or not drying them completely, and talking back to my parents. The belt was worse than my dad's bare hands. My back, buttocks, and the back of my legs withstood the most brutal abuse I have ever known until my marriages. Father's beatings prepared me for the future beatings from other men: a basil skull fracture, attacks with metal objects, and black eyes. My arms were twisted behind my back until the pain brought me to the floor. I have had bruises from chokeholds and purple ears from having my head smashed into bedroom walls. Love to me was distorted. I just didn't know that I deserved kindness.

***

Years later, Dr. Moravic, one of my therapists said, "You know Debra, if a person gets beat long enough, his or her behavior begins to change."

And mine did.

The early abuse took away my self-esteem and self-worth. Pleasing people and making sure their needs were met before mine became a way of living. This behavior pattern was dangerous. Pushing myself further away from developing a sense of self, I never became the woman I wanted to be.

At one point, when I discovered alcohol in high school, my parents sent me to a Catholic priest. Those beers took away the feelings of abandonment and unworthiness. Every time my parents dropped me off at St. Hyacinth's church for a session with Father Mullhern, I looked out the window as our golden Impala drove down Fifth Street. I prayed for the car to turn around to get me. But each time that they dropped me off at the parish, I hastily brushed away a tear. The inferno of abandonment, anger, and resentment turned my cheeks to fire while I begged God to appear before me and make this creepy rectory disappear.

Every other Saturday afternoon, I was in the rectory with Father Mullhern. He knew about as much as parenting as a cardboard box. Nothing.

Mother told me to never tell anybody that they took me to a priest because it would embarrass our family. This was a defining moment for me. It changed the way I felt and what I believed about myself. If my schoolmates ever found out I was sent to a priest, I would never have been able to go back to school.

As for Janie, she was not unscathed. She took a beating I thought would kill her. Mother, father, and I were watching TV. My sister was in our bedroom watching another program. In her excitement, she ran out of the room and changed the channel on our black and white TV. Janie wanted us to see something spectacular she saw. Dad flew out of his chair and took my sister into the bedroom. He beat her to a pulp. Piercing screams filled our house with each punch.

Cowardly, I pulled the blanket over my head and prayed for him to stop.

To this day, I harbor anger at myself for not running into that bedroom, saving her, and beating the meanness out of him.

And of course the words *used goods*. One day after my mother came home from the work at the hospital she told me her friend, Joyce, said that I was *used goods* from my two divorces, which took place in my twenties. My ma said, "Who would want you now?" It didn't matter that those two men physically abused me and sent me to the emergency room on several occasions. What mattered in that "small town" was that I was not the victim but considered the problem. Sadly, some women don't come forward to receive the assistance and help when a domestic violent situation happens.

***

A few years ago Janie recalled what dad had said to her one day.

"I should have never beat you kids like I did," he said.

Those words were never spoken to me.

Maybe if they had, those words might have saved me a trip to the Safe House.

In 1986, I was living in Chicago and married to an abuser.

My parents dropped me off at a Safe House after I called them for help. Refusing to stay there, they took me back to the house in North Chicago. Back into chaos, once again.

Safe House

Gasping my coat collar close to my throat did not stop the cold
November wind from invading what warmth kept my heart beating.
The walk was long; my virgin limp slowed my pace.
Seasoned eyes did not match the young faces
that peered out from behind the tattered curtains.
Faces of White, Black, Purple, Blue, and Green: A race of our own invented by man.
Entering a place of no return.
Why am I standing on their welcome mat?
Painfully, I turn around.
Paperwork shoved into my blood stained hands.
To Serve and Protect sped away, only routine.
Salty tears escaped through the swollen slits of my eyes.
A toothless grin beckoned me in.
A refuge from brutality awaits my story.
A Safe House where no one should ever have to live.

CHAPTER THREE

SO DURING MY senior year in high school, why was my family shocked when I told them I was joining the Navy? I guess they never thought about their actions and behaviors. Actually, my family thought that this is just another one of my outrageous ideas that will eventually fizzle out.

My mother strongly advised me that she would not sign any papers regarding my enlistment. Turning eighteen, I informed her about my decision to join the Navy, whether she approved or not. However, my response did not surprise her. She knew that I was not settling for the quiet and humble life in Peru, Illinois. I was sure that somewhere inside her soul, she felt relieved.

The recruiters eagerly showed up at our door steps to persuade my parents to join the Navy's side. With me as the recruiter's pushy cheerleader, they succumbed to the government's persuasion and mine. They co-signed their names next to my signature for the Delayed Entry Program.

The military was not a way of life for my family. At that time, my father was a factory worker. My mother and Janie both worked at the same local hospital. They were blue-collar workers and dedicated.

For me, life was an escapade.

My heritage is Polish and Irish. I was raised inside the religion of Catholicism.

Baptism, confirmation, communion, and confession are all sacraments and holy endeavors that our family participated in. We also practiced lentil guidelines and did not eat meat on Fridays. We gave something "up" for lent.

In addition, I attended services on Holy Thursdays, Mondays, Wednesdays or whatever day the Catholic Church decided to celebrate meatless days, or a saint's recognition, along with a thirty-minute mass.

Time is crucial to Catholics. The shortest mass in town equals the largest congregation. That makes more time for visiting the tavern after church.

White Way and Sajnaj's Taverns were the local gathering places after mass. These taverns were one block away from St. Valentine's Church. Today, they are still considered monuments in the town of Peru. And what did I get from those thirty-minute masses? The church needed money. I would burn in hell if I got an abortion and if I didn't go to confession.

Every night, I knelt down at the side of the bed and faithfully said the same prayer before going to sleep. "Dear Lord, please watch over my ma, father, sister, and Daisy Dog. I'm sorry for my sins." Then, I recited two Our Fathers and one Hail Mary.

In my teens, I stopped going to confession and started asking questions.

"Mom, what do you get out of mass?"

"Mom, why does the priest always yell at us and then when we see him in the tavern, he's nice to us and Dad buys him drinks?"

"Mom, did you know that the big scab on the Father Chester's forehead was caused from falling down drunk on a vacation in South America?"

My mother replied with the same vague answers, which I did not accept. However, there was one person in my life who answered my questions. And that person was my father's mother, Marie.

"Grandma, why do we go to church and get yelled at?"

"Because of power; it is all about power," she quickly replied.

"Grandma, why are the nuns so mean to us at St. Valentine's Catholic School?"

"Because they don't have boyfriends."

"Grandma, why do I have ashes put on my forehead in the shape of the cross?"

"Because priests smoke just like grandma does and they don't want to waste the ashes."

Janie and I spent a lot of time with Marie when my mother was sick. That was fine by me. Mother and Marie never got along. There was tension in the room when Marie and Mother were together. Marie made statements about the way my mother looked and dressed. They commented on each other's clothes, hair, and of course food. The comments were unkind.

Marie pissed off my mother every time she rode in the back seat of the golden Impala. Grandma smeared the excess Poligrip from her mouth with her fingers to the car seat and back door. Mom cleaned up the pinkish goo after we dropped Marie off at her house. Then, she ripped into my father like a tiger eating its prey. My mother never had a kind word to say about Marie, and Marie never said too much to her but snide remarks. Everyone felt the tension between them.

But I loved being with my Grandma; I felt whole and good and special.

However, the cancer took away the one person I needed the most, my mother. Cancer robbed my childhood and mom's adulthood. Marie took it upon herself to shower her odd influences on Janie and me, adding an essential balance to our lives.

With her wacky jokes and her carefree life style, my Polish grandmother continually fed my passion to treat life as if it was an escapade.

Every time my sister and I stepped in to Grandma's brick home, we were met by the invading odor of cigarette smoke. As soon as we sliced through the white fog, a human chimney sat at the kitchen table watching *The Price is Right*. My grandma.

Marie was the epitome of *Hazel*, the maid for the TV program. She was short and plump. Thin lines of gray weaved throughout her coal, black hair. Her stubby fingers were seldom free of a cigarette. My sister and I scurried to the kitchen table, sat on her plastic-coated chairs, and shouted out prices along with Marie. *Petticoat Junction*, *Green Acres*, Abbott and Costello and Shirley Temple movies, *The Lone Ranger*, *Cisco Kid*, and *I Love Lucy* were among the top shows on Marie's TV agenda.

The Saturday cartoons began as soon as my father left us in her trusting hands. Marie transformed our world into a place where the only tears we shed were because of the bellyaches we had from laughing instead of pain. Our smiling faces never rested from the permanent grins on our faces.

As soon as Marie heard the slam of her son's car door, she wiggled her plump body out from behind the kitchen table and dialed the number she knew by heart. The Yellow Checker Cab Company. This was Marie's means of transportation.

Marie did not drive nor own a vehicle. But if she did, it would be the same model car that was used in the movie, *Chitty Chitty Bang*

Bang. If the car did not fly, Marie would not buy!

The daily preparations for Marie were minimal. Our day of adventure began when Marie took off her flowered housecoat and replaced it with another housecoat. She wore red house slippers. They looked like socks with a flat heel. A swipe of ruby red lipstick, a quick stroke of a comb, and Marie finished her daily routine with brisk sweeps of powdered rouge that she put on Janie's face and mine.

Grandma was the queen of five and dime stores. The employees at Woolworths treated us like royalty as they greeted us. I felt like the people on the grand finale float at the end of the Macy's Day parade.

Everyone in the store waved at us. My sister always sat on Grandma's left side, and I sat on her right. I memorized every joke that Marie told her attentive court.

Grandma taught me many things, such as Bunko, Solitaire, blowing smoke rings, making butter and sugar sandwiches, stretching a penny, and how to irritate your husband in two seconds. But the most valuable lesson she taught me was how to laugh. Even though royalty did not visit her home, she always filled the empty place with the richness of laughter. She gave me two gifts: laugher and dreams. So, a dreamer I became.

Books filled my restless legs with picturesque shores waiting to be walked upon and romantic avenues longing to be strolled on. I could not stop thinking of the far off places I longed to see and to meet the man whose heart could only love mine. Loving me with the deepest part of his heart, I waited with anticipation for that day.

I topped my "Dream List" off with riding an elephant across the sandy coastline of Africa. I envisioned myself wearing a creamy satin scarf wrapped around my head as its tails flirted with the hot breeze. Swimming with dolphins, trekking across Nepal, tasting exotic foods, learning different languages and dance steps, and living with a Polynesian tribe were all on the list.

I wanted to take life by the reins and ride it until I reached the sun in my fearless chariot.

What better way to fulfill my list than by joining the Navy? I could travel to different countries and experience their worlds and mine.

No one could stop the dreams that kept me encapsulated, as I eagerly awaited to step inside of them and begin my journey.

CHAPTER FOUR

ON OCTOBER 1, 1981 at 3:00 AM, I arrived at the Naval Training Command in Florida, stupefied from the past twenty-four hours.

Just yesterday, I was at the bus depot with my family as the Greyhound Bus noisily parked its wide body in front of the Turczyn family. The sliding door opened and waited to ingest me as black curls of smoke escaped from underneath the smelly machine. Hastily kissing my family good-bye, I was swallowed up by the transportation into a new life.

As I sat huddled over, trying to ease the clenching pains that racked across my mid-section, a hand emerged between the vinyl seats. It held a fifth of Southern Comfort. The hand belonged to a fellow by the name of Robert Reese. He was a couple years older than me, and we went to the same high school, but I never really knew him. Michael Osenkarski, Steven Hancock, Mark Riva, Robert Reese, and I were the five area residents heading to boot camp on the same bus. They were going to Great Lakes, Illinois, and I was heading to Orlando, Florida. The burning liquor was a thoughtful and surprising gesture even though it did nothing to calm my nerves.

The bus dropped us off at the Armed Forces Entrance and Examining Station (AFEES) in Chicago for initial processing. Hundreds of bewildered young women and men gathered on the first floor holding their suitcases and waiting for the unknown.

Before the room assignments were handed out, a clinical evaluation was performed. The form consisted of two columns: normal and abnormal. Every body part was examined in this evaluation: pelvic, endocrine, heart, lungs, chest, feet, ears, eyes, vascular, gastrointestinal tract, neurological, and most importantly, a psychiatric evaluation. All of my check marks were placed in the normal column. I was fit for duty.

From the very beginning of my naval career, I learned that "hurry up and wait" was the order of operation for the armed services. Realizing that no matter how fast I hurried up, I usually ended up waiting and waiting. After the extensive medical and psychiatric examination that left no body part untouched, I was handed some white towels that never had the pleasure of mingling with fabric softener. Then, I was sent off to my room.

When I opened the door, there were three other females displaying the same fear on their faces that mirrored mine. I guess the Navy wanted us to get used to the roommate idea as soon as possible. But it did not prepare me for the eighty personalities that I had to bunk with for the next two months during boot camp.

In the wee hours of the morning, I woke up, and quietly used the bathroom first. After I finished bathing and dressing, I walked to my assigned room and waited for orders.

Everyone headed to opposite sides of the country, but the same destination awaited our arrival. Boot camp.

Before we left, the recruits were summoned into a huge room. A sagging American flag sat in the corner. The air was musty and thick as we raised our right hands to take our oaths. Suddenly, my mouth became dry as a peanut butter sandwich. Staring straight ahead, I could not swallow. This was the moment of true commitment. In this murky, drab room among the women and men, I recited the Oath of Enlistment.

"I, Debra Jean Turczyn, do solemnly swear that I will support and defend the Constitution of the United States against all enemies, foreign and domestic; that I will obey the orders of the President of the United States and the orders of the officers appointed over me, according to the regulation and the Uniform Code of Military Justice so help me God. I swear that I am fully aware and fully understand the conditions under which I am enlisting."

The room was silent as everyone absorbed the massive weight of responsibility we were solemnly swore to uphold.

Staring at the American flag, pride wrapped around my beating heart. I was ready to serve.

I had only been away from my family when my childhood friend, Mary Jo Urbanowski, and I slept in her father's camper.

During an eighth grade graduation trip to Washington, D.C., and the times I ran away, were the other occasions.

I realized that on my enlistment day there was no turning and going back home.

I always wondered about what happened to those fellows I rode the bus with that day and where their journeys in the military and in life took them. Did they join the military for the same reasons I did?

I dared to peer out of my childhood window where dreams of escape immersed my vision with fairy tale endings. Did the wine they shared with the golden haired princess disease their blood or did they thirst for more? Did she masquerade her venom with beauty and wrap it around their hearts until no beat could be heard? Did they ever find their happily ever after?

My knights in shining armor used their swords to sever my veins that pumped my heart full of belief. They gallantly dashed away on their frosty, white horses stealing my only fortune: hope.

Did it really matter that I was leaving anyway? This is a question I have always asked myself, because I never belonged to no one.

CHAPTER FIVE

WHEN I ARRIVED in Orlando, ladies from all corners of the United States gathered together and bused to the Naval Training Center Recruit Command, a.k.a., boot camp. At 3:30 AM on October 1, 1981, sleepyheads were awakened by a screaming voice that could shatter the Liberty Bell. This retching voice wanted us to urinate in tiny plastic bottles. She screamed that the reason for this initial test was to weed out the pregnant girls and anyone else whose drug intake happens to exceed "the Navy's Way." The phrase, *the Navy's Way*, was heard over and over again, and that was the last time I was ever given a reason behind anything else we were told to do.

I was assigned to company K001. This group was the first female company to make naval history because this squad was chosen to carry a nine-pound rifle throughout basic training.

My rifle went everywhere with me.

K001 was made up of eighty ladies. Forty women slept on the port side of the barracks, and forty women slept on the starboard side. We lived together under one roof with only eight bathrooms called "the head" in Navy lingo. Frankly, I did not even want to think about "the head" situation in the morning.

The recruiters promised me I would not have to get my long brownish-blonde hair cut. They said, "Nowadays, the female recruits just wear their hair up in a ponytail, as long as it's off their collars."

Unfortunately, so many of their promises turned out to be part of the enlistment game: tell them what they want to hear, which included NOT telling the truth.

Stubbornly, I walked to the barber and sat in his eager chair.

Looking into the mirror, I wanted to barf. My long locks were replaced with short ones, which did not conceal the chubbiness of my face. Both sides of my cheeks looked like jumbo-sized marshmallows were crammed into my mouth for future snacking.

Slowly, the process began: the stripping of my individuality. The Navy placed a banana cap on my head, dressed me in dungarees, black boots, and stenciled every piece of military uniform with my initials, including underwear and bras. I was issued a rifle and a rank. Unconformity was replaced with conformity, as I was turned into a sailor. Reality was finally setting in, but once again, I was bamboozled by my own naiveté.

The K001 company commanders were named Petty Officer Sunday and Stone. These women transformed our civilian world into a military one. Their main job was to convert the recruits' minds and bodies to the Navy's Way. This job was twenty-four hours a day, seven days a week, filled with responsibilities that required patience, scare tactics, and life saving techniques. They were required to turn out top-notch military personnel to be ready at a moment's notice.

On the fourth day of basic training, fear gripped my heart. What did I do? This was insane! Unfortunately, walking up to my company commanders, letting them know I had made a mistake and need to leave right now, I mean RIGHT NOW, was not an option.

Struggling with loneliness, confusion, and physical exhaustion were dealt with within the isolation of the recruits' minds. Nobody in company K001 really knew each another well enough to reach out and express the emptiness we felt. Encouraging words and supportive gestures were neither spoken nor displayed until several weeks into the grueling pits of boot camp.

For the next eight weeks, I was introduced to the most vigorous and physically intense exercise program I have ever voluntarily participated in. The mental training stood right alongside the physical exertion, but it turned out to be far more challenging. The physical drills had to stop sometime during the day, although some days, I never thought they would. But, the mental conditioning or the "head games" the recruits learned to play, never stopped.

From 4:30 AM until 9:30 PM, we were plagued with verbal and mental abuse until, "Yes, Ma'am. I'm a worthless scumbag!" or "Yes, Ma'am. I'll do it the Navy's Way!" automatically sprung from our timid mouths.

Some of the new recruits in K001 did not know how to play the mind games and lost.

Watching one of the girls in K001 lose was an awakening.

She sat stiffly on her bed as if she was made of ice. One human characteristic remained as a tear slid down her despondent face. Everyone in the company pretended not to be watching her as Petty Officer Sunday escorted her away.

I did not celebrate winning the game that day.

Even though I continued to survive, the fear remained right alongside the intimidation. It controlled me so much I was afraid to report the pus filled sores gathering around my ankles. The sores developed from the endless marching and running in my brand new boots.

Petty Officer Sunday noticed I was struggling to get my boots on while the company got ready for inspection. Even then, I could not speak. I was afraid of the ramifications. The look on her face scared me even more. I was given a pass to walk over to the medical clinic and have my ankles evaluated by a corpsman. Petty Officer Sunday did not excuse me from her glaring presence until she unleashed a verbal ass whopping upon me.

Infection began to spread up my legs. After the corpsman's examination, I received antibiotics and a chit (a piece of paper) stating I was allowed to wear civilian tennis shoes instead of boots.

Relief! Happiness sang from my feet as the soft tennis shoes comforted the sores. Oh, the little joys of civilian life I took for granted before joining the service.

Within two weeks, my ankles were back to normal size. Boots became a part of the uniform, once again.

CHAPTER SIX

EVEN THOUGH FEAR was a part of my daily routine, I strived to survive, but this feeling always remained. It just took on a different role and began to motivate me. Excelling in this structured environment so well, I became a section leader during the second week of boot camp. The section included ten women. Soon, I learned that the responsibilities as a section leader were to worry about someone else other than myself. A role I knew well.

My duties included preparing ten women for inspections, keeping gig lines straight, pinning hair up so it did not touch their collars, shining boots until I could see my face looking back at me, checking gear lockers to make sure everything was stowed away properly, listening to complaints, and timing the women's two minute nightly showers.

Our section was prepared and organized for anything that the company commanders literally threw at us. If a recruit's performance was unsatisfactory (UNSAT), then the entire section was ordered to do push-ups, run in place, or hold our rifles out in front of our bodies for an extended period of time. Also, there were the dreaded extra duty assignments.

I could not possibly imagine more duty in boot camp.

The Navy's philosophy behind looking out for one another was the epitome of teamwork.

Fortunately, for my section, teamwork was a concept we learned quickly.

Nevertheless, there had to be an incentive to perform to the best of our abilities. That was the demerit.

Boot camp was based on the demerit system. A recruit could receive a demerit for flunking an inspection, not knowing the eleven orders of the sentry when asked, talking, not asking permission to go to the bathroom, or even walking on the wrong area of the sidewalk. In addition to receiving a demerit, the company commanders also handed out passes to Intense Training (I.T.).

I.T. was the name of this nightly gathering at the central gym. While the other fortunate recruits were studying or writing letters during their half hour of free time, the I.T. invitees were gathered in the gym. After a strenuous day in boot camp, the recruits had physical training and mental conditioning for one straight hour.

If the Intense Training did not straighten up the recruit to the Navy's Way, then she was sent to Cycling. However, at this party, the recruit did not have dance partners to choose from. The recruit and the most sadistic company commander danced cheek to cheek. Once again, I was fortunate that this was one tango lesson I managed to miss.

If these conditioning methods did not work or too many demerits were accumulated, the recruit packed her sea bag and was sent back for one week in boot camp and assigned to another company. Getting set back one week in basic training was an absolute eternity, especially since the recruit had to get to know eighty women all over again.

Watching my fellow service women come back from I.T., Cycling, and then sent to another company was heart wrenching. The disappointment and shame weighed down their physique. The recruits' spirit and dignity crawled into their sea bags along with the rest of their gear, and flung their possessions over their beaten shoulders to be sent back for another week in boot camp.

Courage. Yes, immense courage was what it took to walk past all the women that they began their military journey with but would not finish training together. They said their first good-byes and left us standing there wondering who would be the next one to walk alone.

After eight weeks of boot camp, the last physical test finally arrived. Even though I love to run, this test was difficult because of all the emotions and the underlining fear of failure looming inside my mind.

The test was held in the central gym and a pacer led the pack of eager recruits around the track. The theme from "Rocky" blared from a cheap stereo located on stage. This gesture of music was a good will offering on behalf of the company commander. We had to run five miles on an indoor track. Even though five miles did not seem that far, it was a timed test. A pacer was placed in front of the recruits and we had to keep up with her! If she caught up with a lagging recruit, she tapped her on the shoulder, which meant the recruit failed the test and was sent back for another week of boot camp.

When the pacer stood in front of the nervous recruits, I could not believe my eyes. She was lean and tall like an Olympic athlete. With every step she took, her muscles protruded from her confident frame. What else should I have expected from someone who administered running tests all day long?

Before I knew it, the pacer took off like the trained athlete she was and began the test. We hardly finished two miles when M & M (Marlane Manglicmot) slowed down.

Petty Office Sunday yelled at me, as I cornered the track. "Turczyn, you better make damn sure that M & M makes it! I don't care what it takes. Take care of your shipmate!"

Every time M & M was about to be tapped by the pacer, I fell out from the pack, went back and convinced her that it was in her best interest to move faster and become airborne.

Keeping up with the pacer, I was almost tagged when retrieving M & M. Screaming at her, I felt foolish and mean because she was really trying her hardest. My frustration level kept rising as energy began to decline. I could not stand to see another woman left behind.

M & M did not start out with our company. She had been set back once before to K001.

Thankfully, we all passed the last test that day.

The purpose of basic training was to learn the Navy's Way and to condition the recruit. I learned how to survive in water with only a metal bucket and a pair of dungarees as my life preserver in case I had the unfortunate experience of being thrown overboard. I learned to follow orders without question, put out fires, throw on a gas mask as if it was a baseball cap, and sustain life with nothing but the bare essentials. Also required were First aid, teamwork, naval education, honoring the Uniform Military Code of Justice (UCMJ), operating firearms, folding underwear and bras into tiny squares, and how to put a sheet properly on a bed. I learned to pay attention to the smallest detail because your shipmates' lives depended on it.

The distinct separation of the enlisted service women and men from the officers was clearly brought to my attention during boot camp. The Navy divided us in every aspect of military life:

administratively and physically when it came to base housing, clubs, uniforms, chow halls, fraternization, and respect.

Learning to salute was a class in itself. Anytime I saw gold on a military uniform, I saluted. Gold was everywhere: on shoulders, wrists of the uniforms, leaves on caps, and on the collars of pressed white or khaki shirts. Gold was my superior, and as an enlisted member of the United States Navy, I was obligated under the UCMJ to recognize this supremacy.

Our training was diligently planned and administered to develop character, loyalty, and patriotism necessary to defend our country, its ideals, and people against any aggressor. To obtain these honorable achievements, many personal sacrifices were made that changed the recruits forever.

Graduation day was November 27, 1981. I finally completed boot camp without one demerit. I never flunked an inspection, an academic, or a physical test. Nevertheless, most of all, I met some fascinating women.

My naval career began with one goal: to complete boot camp. Finishing that goal was a great feat.

My parents arrived in Orlando to watch me graduate and to meet their new daughter. But I never appreciated that they took the time to come down to boot camp and see me or the cheeseburger from McDonald's that they had waiting in the car for me. I was still angry with them.

Getting through boot camp was, in many respects, an individual accomplishment. However, the fascinating women of company K001 rightly deserved most of the recognition. Without their social insight, untimely humor, endless guidance, and dedication towards each other, none of us would have made it through those challenging days.

Mary Broadbent, Anna Rose, Peggy Herne, Michelann McIntyre, Marlane Maglicmot, Melissa Parfitt, and most of all, Diane Sneeringer and Artelia Trice, deserve special thanks. Without all of these fine women, I would have never known such camaraderie.

CHAPTER SEVEN

MY FIRST SET of orders was for the Naval Training Command Center (NTCC) in San Diego, California to attend Radioman A School. Seven recruits from K001 had the same set of orders, so we were on the plane together. I do not know how we made our flight because as soon as we arrived at the airport, we fell into the drunken sailor motif. So excited to be away from our grueling hellholes, we celebrated freedom. However, what awaited for us in San Diego was not liberty, to our surprising dismay. We were back in another basic training facility, once again.

Radioman A School was just an extension of boot camp. Still, I contended with the physical training, inspections, and long hours of duty on top of schoolwork. The rules and regulations were strictly enforced. The instructors were just as demanding as our previous company commanders. They thoroughly enjoyed ordering us to drop and give them twenty push-ups or whatever it was for that day. The boot camp methodology kept them amused throughout their long days and added more stress to ours.

Before I entered boot camp, I had to choose a job in the military. Actually, the recruiters suggested the job for me. I was offered a radioman position, and I accept that job offer.

Therefore, I became a Radioman: well, actually a Radiowoman. Radioman A School teaches sailors to learn his or her rate. A rate in the military is a service person's occupation. Once a sailor is in the fleet, she or he can apply for additional training at a C school. I always wondered whatever happened to the B school.

The learning facility was a self-paced school consisting of twelve weeks. The common core of a Radioman was to process and screen messages, operate a teletypewriter, prepare and correct tapes, and to transmit and receive messages. After my interview and a psychological screening with Naval Intelligence Service (NIS), I was approved for a top-secret clearance.

My second goal was to finish school with honors, and thirdly, to get out into the fleet and perform my job. I attended night school to finish classes earlier than the expected twelve weeks.

Within two weeks, I achieved the role of honor student. I earned the privilege to wear civilian clothes, which meant, I did not have to wear a navy uniform every single minute of the day. After months of wearing a uniform, even during down time, I looked forward to utilizing this privilege and working extremely hard to keep it.

Living on the three hours of sleep per night became the Navy's Way for me. I attended classes during the day from 7:00 AM to 4:00 PM, took an hour and a half break, and then went back to the night school until 9:00 PM. I was allowed another break until midnight. Then, I pulled duty from midnight to 4:00 AM. During my breaks, I studied for the next day's assignment. Then I slept for two hours, got up, and started my arduous routine all over again.

Duty was assigned every third day and mandatory physical fitness training was assigned twice a week.

Because my schedule was so chaotic, I hardly had any time to take care of me. In the middle of January of 1982, fatigue followed me everywhere. I woke up tired and went to bed exhausted. Between the headaches, lack of sleep and nutrition, I became ill.

My abdominal region was extremely painful and tender when I touched it. A constant, aching soreness filled my bones.

Hot! My body gave new meaning to the word *hot*. "One more day!" I kept on telling myself. The fear of being sent back to boot camp or left behind, was never far from my mind.

The second night before graduation, I was resting on my bunk. Unknowingly, medically it was the beginning of the end for me. A burning liquid exploded at the bottom of my abdominal region. The pain felt like someone had sliced my stomach open with a knife and poured hot honey into the womb. Paralyzed with pain, I sank into unconsciousness.

The next morning, I woke up in excruciating discomfort all over my body. Forcing myself into the shower, so I would not be late for school, I held onto the tiled wall, trying to ignore the shooting pains coming from the depths of my abdomen. Dizziness flooded my brain. Hunched over in the stall, I tried to wash myself when a stream of brownish-black liquid ran down between my legs.

The absence of self-love and self-worth was a way of life for me. It kept me moving and not thinking. So, onward I go pushing forward.

Standing during morning inspection, sweat slid down the sides of my pale face and the center of my back. After passing inspection, I asked permission to go to the medical clinic on base.

On February 4, 1982, I entered the Naval Regional Medical Center Dispensary. The medical intake interview stated, "An eighteen year-old female complains of pain in her right side for one week. Patient states pain is constant. Palpation it is noted point tenderness to the medical aspect of the patient's abdomen - point tenderness extends 5 cm laterally on the patient's left side and extends laterally to the patient's total right side. Urine analysis and a blood test, CBC, were ordered."

This occurrence was the second time I sought treatment in a military environment. The corpsman that took my medical intake did not treat me like a fellow shipmate. I was not the enemy. His anger and rudeness were especially noticeable when I entered the medical facility. The Navy could not be like this? Not my Navy. Ignoring his unprofessional mannerisms, I wrapped my arms around my stomach, and stood in the line until my name was called.

Meekly, I voiced my complaints with "yes sir" and "no sir" even though this corpsman was not wearing gold. Still, I respected his rank, which was only a couple of stripes higher than mine. He drew my blood, and I gave him a urine sample.

Then, he asked me the date of my last menstrual cycle. Giving him the date, I described the extreme pain in my stomach from the previous night. He waved me away and said to wait in the hallway until the test results came back.

A couple of hours had passed while I stood in the hallway waiting. I wanted to get off my feet and rest!

Finally, the corpsman came out to find me and said, "Oh yeah, your tests results are negative." He tossed me a piece of paper stating that my condition was medically acceptable for transfer.

In disbelief, I wondered what to do next. Getting a second opinion was not an option because it was not required.

Before I walked out, the corpsman smartly added, "I guess you're not getting out of duty today."

I grabbed my cover and left the medical facility. With immense discomfort, I slowly walked back to school. What? Me? Lazy? How dare this man think that I was trying to get out of duty? Maybe these symptoms were in my head, or was I working and studying too many hours? Convincing myself that the flu got ahold of me, I pushed myself through the day.

The Navy had an agenda for me, and I would have done anything to fulfill my commitment. I wholeheartedly trusted the service because I had no reason not to.

Sadly, in the years that followed, this initial sick call turned out to be one of the most crucial diagnoses the medical professionals had missed. Looking back at that girl, as if watching a movie, I can see myself always being afraid to say anything, upset anybody, or do something to ruffle the Navy's Way. Conditioned since childhood, speaking up or acting out meant only pain and disappointment.

I never saw a doctor on February 4, 1982. Also, the laboratory results did not exist in my military medical record. Frankly, I do not think any tests were performed.

CHAPTER EIGHT

ON FEBRUARY 9, 1982, I graduated from Radioman A School and received my first evaluation.

"Seaman Recruit Debra Turczyn's military behavior and adaptability are a direct result of her achievements as a student. She has displayed an excellent military bearing during her entire time in Radioman A School. She familiarized herself with all pertinent rules and regulations and ensured compliance. Her military appearance was always a very positive influence on her classmates. Her demeanor was superlative, and she used available classroom time effectively by completing Radioman A School ten days ahead of schedule. She attained honor student status halfway through the course. Her pleasant personality made her an asset to class moral. Seaman Recruit Turczyn is recommended for advancement and retention when all eligibility requirements are met." J. D. Anthony, LCDR, USN.

Emotions of elation, pride, happiness, and satisfaction rushed through me. The last five days were medically and physically challenging, but my evaluation proved I could do the job even under difficult circumstances. For some reason, I thought it was an awesome accomplishment.

Before leaving San Diego, I was required to fill out a dream sheet picking three places. The choices included geographical duty stations that the new service person got to select. There is a reason why the Navy called it a dream sheet. If a sailor gets the first or second duty station she or he selected, the dream came true.

I choose Hawaii, San Diego, and Australia. They chose San Diego for me. When I joined the Navy, I entered the three-by-three program: three years of active duty and three years of reserve duty, meaning I could spend my entire naval enlistment in San Diego. Or, so I was told.

As soon as graduation ended, I took a taxi to the airport, boarded a plane, and went home to Peru, Illinois. My parents picked me up at O'Hare International Airport. As we drove home, I handed them my first evaluation. Still, I needed their approval! "Great job-we're so proud of you. Well done!"

Always, always, I yearned to hear those words.

Stretched out in the back seat of the golden Impala, the pen mark was still cast on the ceiling. I fell asleep.

Once we got home, mother noticed I was having extreme difficulty sitting. Also, she saw my pasty colored skin and how quiet I was.

I told her what had transpired in San Diego and that the medical service on base told me I was fine. Firmly believing the Navy's diagnosis, I told her not to worry.

February 12, 1982, nine days after my first examination, I was rushed to Illinois Valley Community Hospital because of severe pain in the lower quadrant and heavy vaginal bleeding. There was not a military hospital within one hundred miles of Peru at that time, so I had to go to the nearest medical facility.

I stayed in the hospital for five days and was treated with an IV drip of Mandol: an antibiotic. A pelvic ultrasound and an intravenous pyelogram drip were performed.

The pelvic ultrasound radiology report stated, "A uterus of normal size and shape and free of pathology is seen. The ovaries are easily seen but present no obvious pathology. Conclusion: Essentially normal study."

The IVP radiology report stated, "The preliminary film was unremarkable except for a transitional vertebra on the left. Following injection of dye, there was prompt excretion by both collecting systems, which showed neither blunting nor dilatation. The kidneys were equal in size. Their contours were smooth. The ureters and bladder present no unusual features. Conclusion: Excretory urogram showing no unusual features."

However, the excruciating pain and the bleeding continued.

The discharge summary from the hospital dated February 19, 1982 stated, "The patient was admitted to the hospital with right lower quadrant pain and rather irregular and heavy uterine bleeding. This pain was present when she left the base in San Diego several days before admission to the hospital. She then began heavy uterine bleeding and was seen in the ER and was admitted with probability that it is either a pelvic inflammatory or twisted ovarian or a kidney stone or also the possibility of appendectomy.

The IVP was normal, but she did show clumping blood in the first catheterized urine specimen; however, subsequent straining of the urine did not show any stones. CBC remained within normal range. These reports accompany the patient. White blood cells and differential remained stable HCT (hematocrit-measures percentage of blood volume occupied by the blood cells), and HGB (hemoglobin-the amount of oxygen that carries protein contained within the red blood cells), stayed well despite the rather irregular and prolonged uterine bleeding that she had. A sonogram showed no evidence of any cysts or any abnormality in the pelvis though that this was probably and possible pelvic inflammatory disease as the findings on the physical showed some tenderness on motion of the cervix and sensitivity in the right lower quadrant.

The patient was treated with a Mandol IV for five days. On approximately the third day, it seemed that the tenderness let up and the uterine bleeding was somewhat diminished. However, today the tenderness persists in the right lower quadrant, and the uterine bleeding has continued.

At the present time, I feel that as long as she has a Mandol IV for this length of time, and if the symptoms still persist, a D & C is a possibility and a laparoscopy is indicated." Signed, Dr. W. J. Farley.

Dr. Farley delivered me when I was born, and he was our family doctor for many, many years. Upon his suggestion, I was transferred to the Naval Regional Medical Center Great Lakes, Illinois because I was government property. I needed further testing and possible surgery. Other than the obvious problems, according to the radiologist and the doctor, I needed to be in a government facility for any surgical procedures to take place.

On February 19, 1982, the Peru Ambulance Service transported me to the Naval Regional Medical Center in Great Lakes. Fifteen long and pain filled days had passed since my first visit to a medical facility. I remained in agony and a fog-filled consciousness. Still, I continued to bleed.

My father rode in the ambulance with me to the military hospital. Throughout the three-hour drive, my father kept asking me, "How are you feeling?"

The strained look on my face answered his question even though

I kept telling him not worry. The brave face I had learned to wear so well throughout my childhood and in the military, smiled back at him.

As soon as we arrived at the naval hospital, my father said, "Ma and I'll be back to see you as soon as we can."

Lying on one of the emergency beds, my frightened green eyes watched father's every move. When the time came for him to leave for home, I stared into the same green eyes I possessed.

He gradually walked out and then looked over his shoulder.

Smiling at him I reassured him that I was going to be just fine. A heavy sigh slipped away from me as my father disappeared through the doorway marked "Exit." A tear escaped from my eye. I was terrified.

After a two-hour wait, I was wheeled up to the OB/GYN floor and admitted for observation. A doctor came into my room that night. I had only been in the Navy for four months and felt uncomfortable having a person I normally saluted perform a GYN examination on me.

"Good evening," he sighed between cracked lips. "My name is Dr. Threatte, and I'm going to perform your pelvic exam."

He had black, kinky hair that matched the darkness of his skin. His bulging brown eyes reminded me of an old bullfrog.

The pelvic examination was awful. As he inserted the cold metal pelvic tool into my vagina, the pain was excruciating. As he gently pushed down on my stomach, I screamed.

He immediately informed me that I might have a tubular pregnancy and was going to schedule surgery.

Since I was on birth control pills, his diagnosis was bizarre.

I liked Dr. Threatte because he was the second person to believe in me. Dr. Farley was the first because he transferred me to the naval hospital. Now, this doctor confirmed that something was wrong. Terribly wrong! He knew how much pain and discomfort I was in. Getting validation for my medical condition brought some relief because he really believed that I was sick and not just plain lazy.

CHAPTER NINE

FOR THE NEXT couple of days, I remained in the military hospital with an IV drip filled with antibiotics. On February 21, 1982, Dr. Threatte informed me that he was going to do a surgical procedure called a laparoscopy.

A laparoscopy is a "peek-a-boo" surgery where an incision is made underneath the belly button and above the pubic area. A laparoscope is a thin viewing tube with a magnified lens on one end, which allows the surgeon to look inside the abdominal cavity and view the pelvic organs. In addition, a small amount of carbon dioxide gas is pumped into the cavity through the tube, inflating the patient's abdomen for the surgeon to examine the organs. Tissues samples are collected through the scope for biopsies.

My reaction to this procedure was pure graciousness because I wanted to be liberated from the intense pain that invaded my body for the last month. Just to feel good again and to get back out into the fleet.

I was only eighteen years old. What I would have done back then for a crystal ball to have fallen into my lap and opened my eyes to the future. My sheer ignorance about my reproductive system and health issues kept me silent. Naïve, I was unaware of the reality of my medical situation.

For many years, I blamed myself for not knowing or being involved in these health issues. Since then, I have learned a valuable lesson: to educate and never judge myself about the knowledge that I currently possess but didn't have in the past. And always, to rely on my intuition because it is the internal compass that never takes a wrong direction.

So, I consented to the surgery. Signing my name on the dotted line, I knew nothing about the outcome of this operation.

The night before surgery, a male corpsman came into my room at 11:30 PM. Next to my bed he placed a metal IV stand identical to one I already had. The only difference was the size of the plastic bag hanging from the stand. It was as big as a ten-pound sack of potatoes, and the liquid looked like warm, soapy water.

Ignorantly, I asked the corpsman, "What's that IV for?"

He replied, "Hospital procedure. You have to have an enema before an abdominal surgery."

I thought an enema was a clear, small bullet that felt like a hard form of Vaseline. I did not understand the mechanics of this whole procedure. My blank stare informed him of this lack of knowledge.

He looked at me; half laughed, and said, "You've got to be kidding me?"

As my face flushed, I said, "What are you going to do to me?"

He instructed me about the operation of this foreign mechanism. Taking the long plastic tubing in his right hand, he was going to insert it up my rectum. Then, after opening a valve connected to the plastic bag, the soapy water was to be released.

I was shocked and mortified because this unknown male was going to perform a personal and an embarrassing procedure on me.

I begged him to get a female to insert the plastic tubing in my rectum, but unfortunately for me, the nurses were too busy. Or, so he said. My chances of being spared any dignity was not anyone's concern but my own.

Hands shaking, I grabbed onto the metal bars of the bed and rolled on my side. Shock began to override my fear as the corpsman untied my hospital gown and exposed my nakedness.

He instructed me to separate my butt checks with my hands, so he could insert the plastic tubing. Releasing my hands from the metal bars, I reached behind my back to separate my buttocks. Tears of humiliation and pain ran down my face as he harshly inserted the plastic tubing inside my rectum ripping my flesh. Warm water filled my intestinal tract at an alarming rate. My stomach felt like it was going to rip open from the mounting pressure of the water as it rushed into the intestinal tract.

Stuffing groans of pain into the pillow, the corpsman allowed the water to flow through the tube. My squirming and frantic pleads to stop the pain finally convinced him to seize the torturous procedure. Then, he allowed me to use the bathroom.

Doubled over with gripping stomach cramps, I limped to the bathroom as watery feces ran down my legs. Leaving behind a smelly, black trail before sitting down on the toilet seat, I released a sewage-like odor from the inside of my body and into the bowl.

I remained in that position for the next several hours. Black blood and feces drained out of me until I felt completely exhausted. My sweaty face remained in my hands. I was too ashamed to ever face him again.

By the time I got back to the bed, it was 3:30 AM. I fell asleep only to be awakened by an impatient female nurse. I guess women do work on this floor. She had another IV stand accompanying her with the same size bag I had earlier that night. However, the color of the liquid was burnt orange. The nurse informed me that this procedure, an iodine douche, had to be completed before surgery. She showed me how to operate the release valve, which controlled the flow of the fiery liquid, and to insert the plastic tubing inside my vagina. I was so relieved to be in control of the release valve this time and to have my own hands around my private areas.

I shuffled inside the bathroom and completed the necessary procedure. Even though the douching was as painful as the liquid enema, I gently brushed away my labia and carefully inserted the plastic tubing. This time, the shame of ignorance was not present.

At 6:00 AM, another nurse came into my room. Magically, there seemed to be more than just a few female nurses working the OB/GYN floor. She gave me a shot in my buttocks and instructed me to take off my hospital gown. Even though I did not know why she wanted me to take off my gown or why she gave me a shot, I remained still encased in fear, unable to question anything that was happening to me, especially after last night's violation.

My apprehension level on February 22, 1982, was growing at an alarming rate. My parents had not arrived at the hospital, yet. I gave new meaning to the word *frightened* and wondered about what was going to happen to me next.

As I lay naked underneath the starchy, white sheets, I prayed for my parents and God to show up. I began to feel light-headed as two surgical nurses suddenly appeared. One of the nurses roughly placed a shower cap on my bobbing head. Then, they heave-hoed me onto a mobile cart. They wore caps similar to mine as they whisked me down the hall as fast as their paper elf shoes carried them and rolled my gurney into the elevator.

I must have fallen asleep for a moment. When I woke up my hospital cart had crashed into another gurney. There were bodies everywhere draped with green sheets and shower caps sticking out from under the sheets. This place looked like a morgue.

The nurses tried to park my gurney in between two other patients. They were obviously having a difficult time because they kept banging me into the other gurneys.

Some of the people looked like they were already dead because of their bloodless faces. It seemed like the only sign of life came from the morbid sounds of moans.

My teeth began to chatter from the coldness of the room as my fear escalated.

The pressure in my stomach was excruciatingly painful. After yelling out from underneath my sheet, a nurse showed up immediately to my surprise. I told her I had to use the restroom right now.

She appeared to be annoyed with my request and briefly told me to wait a minute because I was going to be catheterized shortly.

I pleaded with her to let me relieve myself as she left me and returned with a bedpan. I relieved myself in front of these half dead surgical patients. Shoving a metal bed pan underneath me, I tried to urinate on the wobbly cart while covering my breasts with the green sheet, and trying to situate my hand that had an IV needle in it. It was a balancing act I failed.

My physical and emotional well-being did not seem to make a difference to anyone on this hospital staff. Already, a man my own age violated me with the plastic tubing, his fingers, and now this!

Having my naked back and butt exposed to the awaiting patients must have been standard procedure because nobody cared about the protection of my rights. Between the snoring and doped up patients staring at the ceiling, a rushing stream of urine was heard throughout this massive room, as it hit the bottom of the cold steel pan.

A few hours later, two nurses stopped by my cart. One of them said, "Time to go."

They wheeled me into a room, and I was tossed onto a bed that looked like a steel cross. My arms were strapped down and adhesive circles were placed all over my chest, stomach, legs, and arms. Wires were connected to the middle of the circles.

A set of brown eyes appeared over my face. A muffled voice came through his surgical mask. He said, "Are you ready?"

"Ready for what?"

"Another shot."

"Ready for another shot?"

Before anyone responded, I felt like I was being sucked through the bottom of the floor into an abyss of darkness.

***

After the surgery, Dr. Threatte came out to the waiting area and spoke to my mother and Aunt Marilyn. They arrived shortly after I was admitted to surgery because they got lost while driving through the traffic in Chicago.

Dr. Threatte told them, "I have never seen anything like it. Her right fallopian tube was the size of a circus rope. There was a massive amount of hemorrhaging, and she's lucky to be alive. Your daughter must have an incredibly high tolerance to pain. I had to remove her right fallopian tube due to acute and chronic inflammations and fibrous adhesions. After we did the exploratory laparoscopy and found the problem we had to make a six-inch incision in her lower abdomen to remove the fallopian tube. She's in the recovery room now. Once again, I'm sorry that we didn't catch this earlier."

Waking up in the recovery room, I could not find my voice. A white blur of a person stood over me. Ripping off my oxygen mask, I placed two fingers under my nose trying to convey to this blur with the mask on that it felt like I was suffocating. Fortunately for me, this person must have had been great at charades. My oxygen mask was replaced with a nasal-tubing device, and I found my voice.

Peeling open my parched lip, I mumbled, "Where's my baby?"

It is astonishing about how the subconscious mind operates. I blocked out so many personal feelings throughout this whole ordeal, and now they were trying to surface through the powerful anesthetic. Softly, I voiced my concerns.

The white blur was a man. Gently caressing my hand, he quietly whispered, "There was no baby."

He witnessed my operation. My battered reproductive system foretold the death of my future generation. He knew my arms would never hold a newborn child.

CHAPTER TEN

WAKING UP FROM surgery, I was put in a different room. This room looked identical to the other hospital room. It had the same pale old, yellow paint, and gray floor. My heart leaped when I saw my mother sitting on a wooden chair at the end of my hospital bed.

She looked exhausted and defeated just like the many times I saw her as she walked out of the doctor's office in Iowa City and from our return trips from the hospital.

"What is wrong, Ma?"

"Nothing. How are you feeling?"

"I feel awful, but I am so glad that you're here. I was scared before I went into surgery."

"We got lost," she quietly said.

My mother and I did not say too much to one another because I was in a lot of pain. Forcing the conversation was the last thing I had on my mind.

The right side of my stomach felt like a limb had been severed from the rest of my body. The lower quadrant of my abdomen screamed to be rejoined with that limb. It was an incredibly odd sensation. The sharp pains in my chest and stomach made it difficult to breathe.

I found out later that the gas pains were a side effect from the carbon dioxide and/or nitrous oxide pumped into my abdomen during surgery. My rib cage was tightly constricted, as I tried to breathe. Every breath felt like a knife plunging deeper and deeper into the cavity of my chest.

Mom lightly massaged my stomach with downward strokes, hoping to push the gastric air down into my intestinal tract for some relief. She kept on caressing me.

Coming from Mom, this gesture was uncommon but welcoming. She could only do so much because the bandage surrounding my abdomen constricted any movement. It looked like the life preserver water-skiers wore around their waists: heavy and bulky. Finally, exhaustion won over, as I gave up and slipped back into a deep sleep, sparing my eyes from reality.

On February 22, 1982, my post-operative report stated, "Patient was found to have an acute salpingectomy (removal of the right fallopian tube) due to pelvic inflammatory disease. The tube was 6.5 centimeters and a portion of it was terminated by fibrous and hemorrhagic adhesions. Inflammation was acute and chronic with fibrous adhesions."

The following five days in the hospital were repulsive. Something was not right. I could feel it in every inch of my battered body. The lower portion of my abdomen still suffered with a raw, piercing pain. In spite of the fact that my body did not feel like it was healing, I wanted desperately to get back out into the fleet and perform my duties as a Radiowoman. The only positive task I could do was to pray for the healing of my body, and I did a lot of it. I was completely ignorant to any other medical or physical ramifications of what had taken place in that operating room.

While I was recovering, a corpsman was assigned to my care. She happened to be eight months pregnant and annoyed me immensely. Every time she bent over to take my blood pressure or temperature, her swollen stomach brushed against me.

I hated that feeling: a hard stomach reminding me of something I could not grasp onto yet. Her personal hygiene filled my hospital room with a pungent odor. She smelled so badly that my mother had to leave the room every time she walked in to check my vital signs. The nauseating smell never left with her. The order wafted in with the heat from the radiator, causing me to vomit when she left the room. Every time I sneezed, coughed, or vomited, it felt like every single stitch in my stomach was being ripped apart.

On the fifth day, I was released from the hospital on convalescent leave. The Navy granted me thirty days to heal.

What awaited my naïve eyes when the bandages were removed turned out to be a horrifying.

At first, the surgical scar did not seem real to me. Twelve gold clamps pierced through my abdomen creating a smiley face above the pubic area. My skin was bunched up in the clamps just like the outer edges of a homemade apple pie. My shaky finger reached down to touch my stomach, but I could not feel it. The entire area was completely numb. Throwing the white sheets back over my body I squeezed my eyes shut, wanting to avoid the disfigurement of my abdomen as much as possible.

The only procedure left was removing the catheter. A corpsman walked into my room to do this procedure. I even asked for the pregnant female corpsman to remove the catheter, but she was off duty. The staff did not seem to respect the requests of an eighteen-year old enlisted woman who just went through one of the most horrendous surgical experiences in her life.

Removing the catheter was another humiliating experience I had to endure in this hospital. I was facing a young man with my legs spread wide open. This scene went beyond embarrassment at this point. The shame and humiliation were more than any young woman should have to endure.

The corpsman's shaking hands exposed his nervousness. Hesitating, he tried to peel the adhesive tape from my shaved labia, adding to my distress and his. I reached down and pulled the tape off. I didn't want him touching me at all. After several futile and painful attempts, I was finally free from the uncomfortable catheter and his presence.

My family told me that no one could come and get me from the hospital. I was beyond devastated!

Mother told me that the recruiters, who signed me up in the Navy, were in the Great Lakes area, and they would bring me home. I didn't want to go home with them! I wanted my mother.

As 1:00 PM rolled around, a nurse walked into my room and told me I had to leave and wait out in the hallway because they needed the bed. Where was I supposed to lie down? After recovering from major surgery, I could hardly even walk. In intense pain, I grabbed my little white plastic bag containing a few of my items and waited in the hallway by the elevators.

As frustration and abandonment began to rise inside of me, I called my mother on the pay phone. I cried and pleaded with her to come and get me.

She kept on telling me that someone would be there soon.

Once again, I felt like that little girl in the rectory begging God to appear and whisk me away because my parents would not show up to take their daughter home after surgery.

At 5:00 PM, the recruiters showed up. The smell of alcohol swam all around them. The fact that I had to ride home with these heinous people sickened me. Lying down in the back of the van, I held my stomach while tossing back and forth on the long seat. Tears of anger, frustration, and loneliness quietly slid down my face. All the stitches that the surgeons so carefully sewed inside of me began to lose their grip. The searing pain was unbearable. Holding onto my stomach and hugging myself was the only thing that made me feel a little bit better. Why didn't anybody show up? Desperately, I wanted to get out of the van with every stop they made for more alcohol. Worthless-yes. I was not worth anything to no one, not even to myself.

On March 27, 1982, according to my military orders, I had to report to San Diego, California. During my convalescent leave, I did not talk about the surgery, nor did I spend any time reflecting upon it. My first actual duty assignment awaited for me in San Diego, and I did not want to keep the Navy waiting. My job meant so much to me because it gave me purpose and a direction in life. I belonged to something.

An unexpected honor waited for me at the end of my sick leave. I received a letter of appreciation from N.T. Hill, the commanding officer of the Navy Recruiting District Glenview, Illinois.

The letter stated, "On behalf of the Navy Recruiting District Glenview, I take great pleasure in extending my appreciation to you on your tireless efforts in support of One-Navy recruiting. Your selfless contributions of time and resources have contributed significantly to the overall efficiency of this command. The Department of Defense, Navy Department, and the Navy Recruiting Command are dedicated to the realization of the All-Volunteer Force. Your dedication and support are especially encouraging to all of us, as we see men and women of your caliber contribute so fully to this great team endeavor. It is with sincere admiration and respect that I forward the enclosed award and confer upon you the title of honorary Navy Recruiter."

I went back to my high school and spoke with the seniors about the Navy, my expectations, and experiences since I took that honorary oath. I had only been through boot camp and military school, both learning institutions were hard topics to sell. However, when I began to speak, I found myself never at a loss for words. An abundance of loyalty was heard in every word of my speech. My accomplishments and allegiance to the Navy showed even though neither ribbons nor medals were displayed upon my chest. Finally, I felt like I belonged somewhere, to something.

CHAPTER ELEVEN

SAN DIEGO WAS such a mesmerizing city for me. The Naval Communication Station at 937 North Harbor Drive was my new duty assignment. The taxi dropped me off right at the water's edge in front of a massive building. I was expecting to be dropped off at a military base; however, I was not disappointed in my surroundings.

Deep blue waves rocked the sailboats that occupied the marina, as if the sailboats were dancing to an underwater jamboree. The boats' brightly colored flags wiggled from the chilly touch of the ocean's breeze. Birds circled the harbor as fluffy white clouds floated aimlessly in the blue sky.

I asked the taxi driver one more time, "Are you sure that this is 937 North Harbor Drive?"

He looked at me like I was an ignoramus and said, "Lady, I have been driving a cab for a long time. This is your stop."

Walking into the entrance with my green sea bag and brand new carpet-printed suitcase, I winced. My stomach clenched and protested in pain against any physical activity since the surgery. Stopping to rest several times, it felt like something was not medically right with my body.

The directory indicated that the Naval Communication Station was located on the third floor. I took the elevator, got out, and looked around. As I glanced down one of the hallways, I saw a door with a combination lock containing ten buttons and a small mail window to the right of the door. Besides the combination and the window, the whole floor was bare.

Walking back to the elevator, I checked on the luggage I left behind because it was too heavy for me to carry. Leaning against the windowsill, the glorious view of the harbor captured my attention as I wondered what to do. Since this was my first actual duty station, I was a little bit befuddled.

The setting looked more like a vacation spot than any naval base I had ever seen in pictures. I walked back and rang the buzzer next to the door. A woman came to the window dressed in civilian clothes. Right away, I knew I was definitely in the wrong place. I introduced myself and asked if she could possibly direct me to 937 North Harbor Drive. My uniform gave away the reason for the question. She told me I had arrived.

A loud buzzer rang and a door opened up to reveal a colossal communication station. There was a mixture of civilian and military personnel swarming around the area.

The woman led me to the command center and introduced me to the supervisor. He was a civilian, and his name was Bill Rice. I kept searching for a military person to come over and take control of the situation. I looked for superiors to give me my orders.

Mr. Rice was an extremely nice man in his forties. He had dark wavy hair and a kind smile. He told me that since I had checked in on a weekend, I would not be assigned any work or duty until Monday morning. The kind man took my orders and asked one of the workers to give me a ride to 32nd Street-Ford Hall. He may have seen the bewildered look in my eyes and said, "Don't worry. On Monday, the front office will brief you on your duties."

I was elated! Thirty-second Street Ford Hall? Where was I going?

I followed a man downstairs and got into a government truck. Driving down Harbor Drive, we passed an ocean side shopping area, Seaport Village. There were quaint little shops sprawled along the side of the harbor's inlet. The strings led children from their highflying balloons, while their parents strolled behind hand in hand. The village and the ocean complemented one another.

The twenty-minute ride to Ford Hall was invigorating. The ocean never left my view. As the driver and I approached 32nd Street, mammoth vessels were lined up all in a row as if standing at attention to welcome my arrival. These vessels were my first trifle glimpse of the Navy.

Goose bumps raced down my arms and legs from the overwhelming size of this impressive gray fleet. My adventure had finally begun.

CHAPTER TWELVE

I CHECKED INTO my new residence on the outskirts of 32nd Street on March 27, 1982. A brown, wooden fence surrounded the military barracks like a fortress, but they looked just like any other ordinary apartment buildings. I got out of the government truck, thanked the quiet man, and walked up to Ford Hall.

Blindly, I just kept walking forward. Where to go? Or what to do? All of these questions. This setting was such a contrast from my first four months in the Navy because it was not so sterile.

I walked into the front office and stood on the quarterdeck. A real quarterdeck is found on a ship and functions as the welcoming and departing hub. The main building at Ford Hall was considered the quarterdeck of dry land and the processing area for my housing assignment.

Many military people wandered in and out of the quarterdeck checking out the new "wave" checking in. Women in the Navy are called waves or winds. I dislike these terms.

The Petty Officer on duty briefly gave me a run down on the rules and regulations of Ford Hall. Then, he moved on to the most important thing that was pressing on his small mind, like my marital status. Of course, having "fresh lamb" written across my forehead, I smiled in delight at this Petty Officer who noticed me.

I was assigned to the corner room on the third floor of Ford Hall. Grabbing my bags, I went to search of my new room, only to be forced to my knees from the throbbing pain in my stomach. The pain wrapped around my body and collided into the center of my back. Keeping my brave face intact, I forced myself to push forward.

I did not want to show any signs of helplessness to warn my fellow service members that I was momentarily a fragile piece in this steel Navy.

The barracks were U-shaped with three wings surrounding an open centered plaza. In order to get to my room, I had to cross the center of Ford Hall. While I was trekking across the concrete plaza, whistles and coyote howls welcomed my arrival. Marines! They were everywhere, as I looked up to the third floor of the balcony. They were hanging on the steel posts performing acrobatic stunts to amuse the women or themselves.

Climbing three flights of stairs, I quickly found my room on the west wing, which was occupied with marines. I was getting to like these charming, yet wild men that tried so hard to get my attention.

Opening the door to my room, I saw a woman sitting on her bed in a haze of smoke. She reminded me of my grandmother, Marie. The woman's cigarette dangled from the corner of her mouth.

Coated in a southern drawl, she quietly said, "Hello," without taking her eyes off the book she was reading.

As another woman popped out from beneath her bed covers, a familiar face met mine. Peggy Hearne.

She was in my boot camp company, K001. We attended military school together, and now we were roommates, once again. A huge sigh of relief escaped through my lips, as I finally got to sit down on my bed.

On Monday morning, I checked into the Naval Communication Station on Harbor Drive and began my new career. However, one administrative error appeared on my naval orders.

I joined the Navy on a three-by-three program: three years active duty and three years inactive duty (reserves). My date of rotation in my military records was stamped March 1983.

The Chief of Personnel told me, "It seems as if someone made a mistake in your orders when that someone typed them up. You should be stationed in San Diego for eighteen months, not just for one year at this command center. Rotating before fulfilling your obligation is illegal."

A look of distress immediately washed over my face.

Then, he added, "Don't worry I'll have this incorrect date changed before you are due to transfer."

I blurted out, "Are you sure? Are you really sure?"

"Yes, yes, don't worry. I promise to take care of this error."

As a watch stander at the telecommunication center in San

Diego, this automated message-processing site, which provides telecommunication services to over two hundred major shore commands and afloat units, and processes over two hundred thousand messages a month, became my home.

I worked during the peak load hours, which were the busiest hours of the day in a communication center. This environment was alive with noise, shuffling of papers, and people running around trying to get vital messages to the designated ships and shore stations.

The only concern that hovered over me like a shadow was my health. Still, I did not feel well after my surgery. Fatigue followed me everywhere.

During the first week in May of 1982, I began to experience light-headedness. My energy level dropped significantly, and the weight packed onto my hips, stomach, and thighs. Feeling like a puffed out blowfish, and to my dismay, I looked like one. I went to the Naval Regional Medical Center Balboa in San Diego.

I was hospitalized on May 12, 1982 for gynecological problems from my surgery. A message was sent to my duty station stating that I was to be hospitalized for six to ten days.

The hospital was different than any other one I had ever been in. Twenty beds were lined up in the middle of the gigantic ward. Another twenty beds were behind them. The headboards of the beds were back to back. The only privacy the patients had was a curtain.

Gender did not matter on this ward either. Males and females occupied the beds. Seeing a personal doctor in this hospital was like hitting the lottery. A team of white-coated men came and visited me every other day. Someone from the team picked up the hospital chart that rested on a hook at the end of my bed, glanced at it, and placed it back on the hook. There was an air of haughtiness that encompassed this team every time they stopped by my bed. Because fear and intimidation were instilled in my mind, I did not ask any questions. What questions was I supposed to ask? Angry with myself for not knowing anything about my condition, I just sat on the bed and stared right back at the team. My fortress of comfort and support never existed. I was alone in trying to figure out the medical maze I found myself in.

The aura of supremacy was daunting. How I wished a family member would have been there to question the military team's actions or treatment. Once again, I naively thought these officers would take care of my ongoing condition. After all, they were doctors, right?

On the third day of my hospitalization, a corpsman informed me that a sonogram would be performed on my abdominal region. The pre-procedure process consisted of drinking several glasses of water. The pressure in my stomach was unbearable with every glass of water I drank.

When a corpsman advised me that it was time for my test, unfortunately, they were short staffed, so I had to escort myself to radiology.

Back in 1982, Balboa Hospital reminded me of an aged building fighting to exist. It was not an entirely enclosed facility. The exposed stonewalls and stairs seemed like an ancient castle. Trying to find the way to radiology while hooked up to an IV, I bumped into dead ends while maneuvering myself through the maze after many unsuccessful turns and going in the wrong direction. After finding the radiology department, I ascended the stone stairs while dragging my IV stand behind me.

Inside the sonogram room, a male corpsman was listening to loud, heavy metal music.

I yelled out my name.

Screaming back at me, he told me to wait while he got the room ready.

The corpsman was extremely hyperactive and anxious. He kept on asking me if I had drank enough water.

I told him, "Yes!" five times. To this day, I strongly believe he was on some type of stimulant because of his whacked out behavior.

"My time and the Navy's time will be a complete waste of time if you didn't drink enough," he smartly yelled above the blaring music.

The mounting pressure from drinking so much water made me want to rush to the bathroom. The heavy metal music still blared as he shouted impatiently that he could not hear me.

I screamed at him, "I have to use the bathroom!"

"Just get up on the table and pull your underwear down around your knees," he scolded at me.

He poured a vast amount of clear jelly over my swollen abdomen. The sonogram machine was a half sphere, about the size of child's rubber ball.

As he moved the cold ball back and forth over my belly, the pressure felt like my bladder was about to burst.

"I need to go the bathroom now. I can't stand it anymore!"

"Just wait. I'm almost done!" he hollered back at me.

I winced back the pain, but could not hold back the mounting pressure any longer.

"Please, I desperately need to use the bathroom!"

"And I told you to wait. I need to get a good reading!" he sputtered back at me.

As he spoke those harsh words, my weakened bladder gave in to the pressure. At first, I felt the dampness of warm urine seeping through my hospital gown. The yellow and bloody liquid spilled off the table and onto the floor beneath me like a waterfall. I lay on the wet table immersed in utter shame. Relief and embarrassment washed over my entire body at the same time.

Needless to say, the corpsman was not happy with me as a few choice words flew from his mouth.

Slowly, I swung my shaky legs off the wet table and left. A small stream ran down my legs, as I hobbled away.

Turning, I watched him recklessly throw white towels all over the table. He never offered me one because he was not even aware that a breathing human being had just left his precious, cold, and lifeless table.

Shuffling back to the ward in a deep state of depression, I didn't care who saw the ring of wetness that encompassed my entire rear end. A solemn trance encased and protected me.

On May 17, 1982, I was released from the hospital. The doctor's note stated, "Please be advised that Debra Jean Turczyn should remain in S.I.Q. (sick in quarters) for twenty-four hours from 17MAY82 to 18MAY82. Thank you. If you have any questions, feel free to call." J.W. Match, M.D.

Feeling awful, I returned to the hospital. The same symptoms continued to persist. Sitting was painful, my abdomen was extremely bloated, and the chronic fatigue never subsided.

Again, I was given another note. It stated, "She is capable of full-time work but hours should be limited to eight hour days, forty hours a week, and prolong standing and lifting should be avoided." Thomas R. Poore, LCDR, MC, USNR.

Releasing me and sending back to full duty? Really? Something was terribly wrong inside my body, and I could not get anyone to listen to me.

I phoned my mother from the hospital and told her that the doctor sent me back to work, but I still did not feel well.

She didn't know what to do, and neither did I.

Forward march! What else could I do? I did what everyone else was doing in the Navy. I ignored me.

However, two things kept me motivated and focused throughout the excruciating pain: a trip home in July for a vacation and a card I received from my dad on June 18, 1982.

Our family always took a family vacation during the last two weeks of July. This year we were going to Kalfran Resort on the Lake of the Ozarks. We went there last year before I enlisted in the Navy. I can't believe it had only been a year and so many things had already happened to me on my journey.

The card my dad sent me had a picture of Gonzo, a Muppet character, on the front of it. Several other Muppets surrounded Gonzo and he said, "Without you…I feel lonely even when I am in a crowd! Miss You!"

I opened up the card and there was a hand written letter from dad; the only letter he has ever written to me in my entire lifetime. My mom was the card sender and letter writer. For the first time, he opened up a part of himself and placed it inside of this card. I never knew this man to be my father.

I was shocked by the words in the card, and over the years, I have kept it in a protective plastic baggie. The words my father wrote seemed so disingenuous to me because I always felt like a nuisance, in the way, or someone that he had to put up with because I was his daughter. Somewhere inside, my father was a tender man. A tenderness that needed to be healed, too.

"Hi Deb, how are you? I just took Ma to work, so I thought I better write you a few lines. It's early in the morning, and Matt (my nephew) is sitting in his butler chair by me. He's trying to talk to me, and he says, "Hi" to his Aunt Deb.

Matt is cutting teeth again, and he's a little crabby. Janie and I are going to take him to the doctor today because he has a little cold.

Everything back home is ok. My chest cold is all cleared up, and I'm feeling better. Sundstrand is closed down again for two weeks from June 14 to June 28. The recruiters want to have a party for you when you get home. How is the old Chevy running? Ok? Did you get the grease and the oil changed yet? Don't forget to have the oil checked when you get gas. Janie and I are having a garage sale tomorrow. We've been rounding up Gary, Matt, Janie, and Ma's clothes, and yes, even yours. Just the clothes that don't fit anymore. I'm taking everything that doesn't move and selling it! Ma isn't even having a fit! We are going to split the money and use it for our vacation.

I am sure glad that we are going back this year again because we had so much fun in Missouri the last time we were there. Also, I'll have my family together again for vacation, which will make me VERY HAPPY! Janie and Matthew cannot wait. We'll be talking to you on the phone.

Love, Dad.

P.S. Thank you for the Father's Day card. When I opened it, I started crying. It really made me feel good. Love you a lot, Dad. XXXXXXXOOOOOOOO."

CHAPTER THIRTEEN

July 1982

AS SOON AS the plane landed in Chicago, I walked out of the terminal. My parents rushed me up to Great Lakes Naval Regional Hospital because they knew that something was terribly wrong, too.

When I was called into the OB/GYN exam room, I found out that Captain Myers and Dr. Threatte were assigned to my case, again.

I met Captain Myers briefly the first time I had surgery at Great Lakes. His grandeur took command of any room he waltzed into. He carried his height like a feather. Immediately, he recognized me and softly engulfed my hand with his massive one.

The doctor examined me, and to my disappointment, he gave me another round of antibiotics. With a heavy heart, I could not believe that Captain Myers had given up on me, too.

Quietly, I left his office and met my mom and dad in the waiting room. My sagging shoulders and long face gave me away. I told my parents that it was just another round of antibiotics, another futile attempt at dismissing me.

My mother's face turned to stone as dad placed his confused head into the palms of his hands. Grabbing her vinyl purse and stuffing it harshly under her arm, she marched through the exam room and right into Captain Myers' office. She ignored the military nurses' commands to go back into the waiting area.

A few minutes went by before I was called back into the examining room as two nurses escorted my mother back to the waiting area.

I sat down on the hard wooden chair next to his enormous desk.

He sat back and starred at me, a fountain pen tucked between his head and ear. His sparkling, white uniform and four gold bars adorning both of his broad shoulders frightened me. I saw him as a Captain in the US Navy and not a physician anymore.

The silence became louder, as I could not take my eyes away from his. I needed his help.

"I'm going to do an exploratory surgery with the possibility of a hysterectomy," he cautiously told me. He grabbed a book from a shelf amassed with hundreds of medical texts and opened it up to a page displaying the female reproductive system.

"Do ever want to have children?" he asked.

I, with all of my nineteen years of youthful wisdom responded, "Sir, I will do whatever it will take to feel better again, so I can get out into the fleet and serve. I have to get back to my duty station."

Not one man, captain, or even a doctor should ever propose such a question to a young lady who doesn't have the knowledge of motherhood or what it feels like to bring life into this world. I wonder what the answer would have been after a woman experienced a hard labor? Would the same question have been asked of a man before an orchiectomy (removal of the testicles)? Or even if the question would have been proposed at all?

In those five minutes, I was not thoroughly educated by the picture book Captain Myers showed me. How could I have been? Frankly, I didn't even know how my reproductive system functioned even after a high school health class. I wasn't paying attention back then.

Many people, including my parents, had difficulty explaining sex and the reproductive systems of the male and the female to their children. Unfortunately, during the 1970's, the norm was NOT to talk about sex with your parents. I never had "the talk" or really knew what to do when I began my menstrual cycle. Self-taught was the name of my teacher.

Hormones! I did not know the importance of those precious little messengers that were secreted into my body, and how they affected the body, and more importantly, the mind. Since I began my menstrual cycle, I had never experienced any problems.

Hysterectomy was a foreign word with a positive solution for me to stop the chronic pelvic pain, fevers, the searing pain in my lower abdomen, and to rid myself of the exhausting feeling that engulfed me.

Before I left his office, he informed me that signing a simple, white piece of paper, gave the surgical team authorization to perform any procedure that was deemed necessary to sustain life.

"Signing this document is standard procedure," he informed me.

Following orders, and to relieve myself of this agonizing pain, I signed my name on the dotted line, once again. Only this time, I gave away my birth rite.

A message was sent to the Naval Communication Station in San Diego stating that I will be hospitalized for an estimated period from five to seven days.

My parents sent another message from Western Union to the Commanding Officer at the Naval Communication Center in San Diego: 'Attention CWO2 Evans: Debra Jean Turczyn emergency admission to the NRMC Great Lakes Emergency surgery.'

I went through the iodine douche and enema regimen again. But this time, I performed the procedures without the aid of a corpsman. Keeping human dignity that was not afforded to me during my previous hospitalizations was important to me.

Today, I look back at that obedient young woman sitting in the bathroom all alone, inserting plastic tubes into her body. I weep for her trembling hands and her quite concerns that went unanswered. I weep for the loneliness and sorrow that was buried deep inside her heart in a room called fear and denial. She traveled this unknown journey without anyone to shade the silent tears falling from her face.

CHAPTER FOURTEEN

I WOKE UP in a regular room this time instead of in recovery. As I peeled my eyes open, an unknown woman stood hesitantly in the doorway. She was draped in a white hospital coat, had a stethoscope around her neck, and her blonde hair was pulled back into a messy ponytail. Her forehead was scrunched with wrinkles, as she appeared to be cautious. She introduced herself as an observer of the surgery. In a nervous voice, she asked to come in, and I nodded.

She wanted to see how I was recovering after spending such a long time on the operating room table. "My name is Megan, and I'm a pre-med student here at Great Lakes Naval Hospital. I'm doing my internship here."

I asked, "What happened to me in there?"

Politely ignoring the question, she replied, "I was only in the observation room. Some other students may stop by to see you, too." Megan touched my arm and gave it a gentle squeeze. "You are a brave, young woman." Then, she left just as quietly as she appeared.

The lingering anesthetic took control of my eyes and closed them for me. Sleeping was an invitation I rapidly accepted.

Everyone inside that operating room witnessed the death of my future generation. Children.

Dr. Threatte met my parents after surgery and said, "I performed a total hysterectomy. I had no other choice. Her threshold of pain far exceeded any patient I have ever seen."

My medical records described what the military doctors found on July 30, 1982.

"The preoperative diagnosis of chronic pelvic pain. The operative findings were a left ovarian cyst and pelvic adhesions. The specimens that were taken were her left fallopian tube, ovary, uterus, cervix, and cicatrix (recently formed connective tissue on a healing wound, scar tissue). Sections of the ovaries demonstrate a hemorrhagic corpus luteum."

ADMITTED: 29 July 1982 DISCHARGED: 4 August 1982

Patient's History: "This nineteen year old, white, female, with a last menstrual period of July 15, 1982, was admitted complaining of lower abdominal pain since May when she was hospitalized in San Diego and treated with antibiotics with little response. She is currently on Vibramycin. The patient was on oral contraceptives until June 1982. The patient is status post laparotomy in February of 1982 as the Naval Regional Medical Center found the patient to have an acute salpingitis with pyosalpinx. The patient underwent a right salpingectomy at that time and the patient subsequently responded to triple IV antibiotics of Cleocin, Gentamycin, and Ampicillin. The patient is an active duty female station only at San Diego to the present. The patient denies alcohol, tobacco, or drug abuse. She has a noncontributory family history. She had a tonsillectomy at the age of seven years old. Her adult illnesses were limited to pelvic inflammatory disease, which is described in the present history. She is status post tonsillectomy and right salpingectomy. She has no injuries and no history of allergies.

Her physical examination revealed a well-nourished, well-developed, white female in no acute distress that was oriented, cooperative, alert with memory grossly intact. The neck was supple. The chest was symmetrical. The lungs were clear. The breasts were without masses or discharge. The heart was normal sinus rhythm, nor murmurs. The abdomen is soft with bilateral lower quadrant tenderness and the pelvic examination revealed the external genitalia to be within normal limits, and the uterus to be anteverted, normal size and painful upon mobilization and palpation. The adnexa were bilaterally tender. The extremities were without varicosities or edema."

HOSPITAL COURSE: "On the day after admission, the patient was taken to the operating room, underwent an exploratory laparotomy, and patient was found to have pelvic adhesions with a left ovarian cyst and a left pyosalpinx. The patient underwent a total abdominal hysterectomy with left salpingo-oophorectomy. The patient's postoperative course was uneventful, and the patient was discharged with recommendation for convalescent leave, fully ambulatory on the fifth postoperative day to be seen in the

OB/GYN Clinic in four weeks.

FINAL DIAGNOSIS: Pelvic Adhesions

AD: Left Ovarian Cyst

AD: Left Pyosalpinx

SURGICAL PROCEDURES: Exploratory Laparotomy

Total Abdominal Hysterectomy

Left Salpingo-Oophorectomy

The patient was discharged as above. No permanent disability is anticipated."

J. Threatte, M.D.

APPROVED: R.C. Myers, CAPT, MC, USN

Chief, OB/GYN Service

Naval Regional Medical Center, Great Lakes, Illinois.

***

After my second surgery, the doctors told me that a small portion of my right ovary was left in during the first surgery. However, my medical records stated, "sections of the ovaries demonstrate hemorrhagic corpus luteum."

***

Captain Myers walked into my room, leaned against the windowsill and stared out the window. "We left a small portion of your right ovary in, and it should take care of the estrogen supply."

Confused, I looked at him.

He kindly explained, "Even though you only have a small portion of your right ovary, it will supply your body with the necessary estrogen."

"But I thought my right ovary was taken out in the first surgery because my fallopian tube was so infected that my ovary was, too?'

He didn't respond. Then, he spoke about the weather, and my upcoming trip back to San Diego. He said that he loved the changing seasons in Illinois. The seasons reminded him that life was coming and going.

"I love the warm weather and the sound of the ocean's waves crashing down upon the shore," I said.

As the doctor walked out the door, he grabbed a toe from underneath the starchy hospital sheet, and wiggled it. "Take care," barely escaped from his lips, as he exited the room.

I did not know that a portion of an ovary left behind that is not attached to a fallopian tube usually ends up dying from the lack of blood supply. It was just floating inside, in right field, so to speak, not attached to anything. Many disastrous complications can occur when an ovary is disrupted due to a medical procedure such as mine. Not knowing one aspect about estrogen, I kept pushing forward.

First, I want to make some points perfectly clear. I do not blame the physicians at the Naval Regional Medical Center in Great Lakes for the end result: sterilization. I came to the NRMC Great Lakes because of the neglect and actions from other naval physicians and medical staff members in San Diego. Both times when I arrived at the NRMC in Great Lakes were due to extreme emergencies. The other naval physicians and staff members in San Diego did not do what they were sworn to uphold, to give the best medical care to their patients.

Secondly, the San Diego physicians never gave me the consideration that I might be telling the truth about my symptoms. Nor did they treat me like a patient with a serious medical problem. Unfortunately, this would not be the last time a naval physician or a staff member excused these deep concerns about my health.

Each time I arrived at NRMC Great lakes, my internal organs were damaged and diseased. NRMC Great Lakes was NOT the station I was assigned to; San Diego, California was my duty assignment. Captain Myers and Dr. Threatte did what was medically necessary to save my life, considering what damaged organs laid in their hands.

There was one other person who was responsible for saving my life. Without her, I would have bled out. I was septic at that point. That person was my mother, Bernadette Jean Turczyn.

If it had not been for her stubborn insistence and clever maneuvering to get me inside the examination room to speak with Captain Myers, I would have walked away to my death.

No military wall or the Navy's Way kept my brave, civilian mother from voicing her deep concerns about me.

Today, I know that I had an unnecessary hysterectomy. My obvious medical symptoms were not taken seriously while I was stationed in San Diego. Too much time was wasted. The misdiagnosis, such as laziness, was not a reason for my persistent illnesses.

Numerous options and procedures could have been performed before any of my organs were left to die. Why weren't these other options available to me?

Initially, my physical recovery accelerated at a rapid pace. I began to lose the weight and the bloated body. Sitting, walking, and running became a part of my daily routine again without feeling like every movement was like a sharp knife that was stabbing my belly.

I felt good to be alive again. I acted like an energetic nineteen-year old for the first time.

Again, I was told by the military doctors, "You are lucky to be alive." However, there was one more abdominal surgery waiting for me in a few more years. It lurked in the background waiting to take my life, one more time.

I never acknowledged what took place in that operating room. Denial gradually washed away as acceptance came into perspective. Once the unfolding of the armored layers I had wrapped around myself during the emotional and physical medical journey began to lose their resistance, a festering, penetrating element appeared: the truth.

April of 1993, eleven years after all of my surgeries, I began to realize and feel the emotional pain of being sterile.

Lullaby

I search in the questioning eyes of the youth wondering –
Where did my children go?
What gender you may have been is not important to me.
The gift of life would soothe my maternal need.
I will never witness the warm Christmas glow upon your round, little face.
Nor kiss away tears of sadness from life's broken dreams.
Vacant are the stages in your school plays.
No graduation cap to throw.
Not a single toast on your wedding day.
Hungry are my arthritic arms for your tiny newborn.
My passage in this life will leave no future, for I am the end.
Can someone please sing a Lullaby for me when I am laid to rest?

CHAPTER FIFTEEN

I RETURNED TO San Diego in early September and went back to work. Upon arriving in San Diego, I was a Radioman Seaman Recruit E-1 (RMSR). The enlisted ranks begin at E-1 and end at E-9. In order to be advanced in the enlisted ranks, military personnel must complete certain requirements, courses, and exams.

Basic Military Requirements (BMR's) and Personnel Advancement Requirements (PAR's) are designed checklists for advancement. This list demonstrates the sailors' abilities in their occupational rating, local commands recommendations, and passing the advancement examinations.

On April 16, 1982, I was advanced to E-2, and on October 16, 1982, to E-3 after completing the naval education training requirements. I was never concerned about my rank because working for the Navy was an enjoyment for me. I knew my job extremely well, even though my naval career was interrupted several times within the year. I kept up with my training and job responsibilities in spite of my surgeries.

There were eight rotating positions within the communication station. One of my favorite jobs was courier/driver. No one really liked driving in San Diego because it was tedious, physical, and carried a lot of responsibilities. The driver had to pack up all of the narrative traffic within the last twenty-four hours that was sent to the communication center, and then deliver it to the surrounding naval bases and ships. Preparations for these highly sensitive documents took two hours and delivering the narrative traffic took an additional two hours.

The bases and ships were spread out within a fifty-mile radius. I loved driving around San Diego at night, meeting new people, and visiting different bases. Driving kept me close to the ocean.

Before starting work at 4:00 PM, I spent time on Coronado Island swimming, body surfing, and admiring the vast ocean stretched out before me. The water invited my adventurous mind to sail perilous voyages of its own whimsical desires. I felt mesmerized by the ocean as if it was a mythical deity seducing me with its passion of whirling waves.

While driving at night, I gazed upon the shimmering, midnight blue ocean, anticipating tomorrow's reunion. Nature truly offered comforting arms to turn to.

I volunteered for that position many times. It got me out of the enclosed communication station and away from the politics. Getting into the small government truck and driving to Point Loma, 32nd Street, the Naval Training Center, Marine Corps Recruit Depot (MCRD), and the submarine base, gave me freedom. But this journey was to end soon.

During the month of October 1982, I had a surprise waiting for me back at the station. It left me confused. The Naval Personnel Department called my command center and told my supervisor that the chief wanted to see me in his office. Many people in the military look up to the chief because he or she earned this rank and has vast knowledge about the military.

When I walked into his office, the chief could not look me in the eyes. He told me I was due for a rotation in the March of 1983.

Puzzled, I stared at him and said, "Chief, you told me upon my arrival at this command station that if I was to leave this duty station before eighteen months of fulfillment, leaving will be considered illegal by the Navy's standards. I have only been here seven months. How can I legally rotate?"

He replied, "I didn't realize that your time to rotate came so soon."

The administrative action necessary to correct this error was beyond his repair. He told me that I had to rotate because too much time had gone by in order to fix the problem. I must follow orders.

Finding his excuses and answers unacceptable, I kept my mouth shut and sat down in disbelief. The promise he made to me earlier in the year about taking care of this illegal error never came to fruition.

"There seems to be another problem here," he proceeded to tell me.

"You are assigned to the pacific realm, so your next duty station will have to stay within that geographical location. You will be assigned to a position or a ship. Naval regulations state that the mandatory requirements of stay is at least two years at an overseas assignment or a little less time depending on the location of the duty station."

Ignorantly, I told the Chief of Personnel, "Well, that's impossible because I only have eighteen months left in the Navy."

Suddenly, the sky of reality opened up and poured its light upon me. "You mean I have to sign up for an extended stay? Are you telling me I'm not getting out of the Navy in 1984 like the recruiters told me?" Nevertheless, I did not give him time to respond. I turned to leave his office as too many unknown situations rushed through my besieged brain.

"Seaman Turczyn, you have not been dismissed. Sit down and listen to me! We have a lot of paperwork and swearing in that we have to do, again. You are in the Navy now, and you have to play the Navy's Way," he strongly advised. "Besides, what's an extra two years of your life? Here are your choices: Hawaii, Australia, Japan, Alaska, Guam, and Diego Garcia. Here's the number to call Washington D. C. You might want to call your detailer; he or she may be able to help you."

"Detailer? What's that?" I immediately asked him.

"You've been in the Navy eleven months, and you don't know what a detailer is?"

My blank expression answered his question.

A detailer was a person who handles your duty assignments, kind of like a travel agent who works for the government.

Then, I realized that the clerk did not made a mistake on my initial orders to San Diego; this detailer person did. So now, I had to call up this inefficient person and thank her or him for not correcting the error. Secondly, I had to ask for a great duty station. I decided to leave out the first round of sarcasm and move right onto gratitude.

As I left the chief's office, I felt an overwhelming sense of panic. I had my naval career all planned out and was in control of my own destiny. After signing that three-by-three contract, I really believed the agreement would not be broken. My gullible mind was beginning to learn that I did not own a single piece of myself. I should have learned this lesson when the Navy removed my internal organs. The word government property dictated my physical being.

After doing some research and asking many questions, I found that staying in the pacific area could be avoided if I volunteered for a special assignment. Options! Yes, I will take them!

The door to an exciting world opened with embassy duty. Exploring the possibilities, I wondered about what to do for the rest of my life. I began to think the Navy's Way. Rank became a concerning factor now, and the possibilities of remaining in the military for twenty years became an option I wanted to grab onto.

After many hours of sitting on the beach and staring into waves, I contemplated the negative and positive aspects of different duty stations, staying in the Navy, and making it my career. I wanted a position that was interesting, different, and showed initiative in my service record and most importantly, to serve my country. Recalling what the chief had stated, "Once you are overseas, there's no coming back state side until you have fulfilled an additional tour; back-to-back duty."

In 1987, I would return stateside once again. For five years, could I stand to be away from American soil?

My enlistment began with three years, but I decided that day, on that beach, in Coronado Island that I would give more than eight years of duty for my country. My life will be the United States Navy.

CHAPTER SIXTEEN

EMBASSY DUTY WAS an elite position. However, I could be stationed in an embassy in Beirut. Nevertheless, I remained loyal and steadfast to my enlistment oath. Even though fear and excitement ran side by side, I pursued a new direction in my life. Still, my faith and commitment to the Navy far outweighed other emotions that dared to race with me.

Disappointedly, all the embassy positions, which are called billets, were filled. My Detailer told me that there was something else that I could apply for: MAAG/MISSIONS: NATO.

On October 14, 1982, I filled out a chit and respectfully requested consideration for MAAG/MISSIONS: NATO. Once it was approved, my new duty station was revealed to me.

November 9, 1982, I received orders from Washington D.C. On March 20, 1983, I was going to be transferred to the Allied Forces Southern Europe, Naples, Italy until April of 1985. The Navy added an additional eight months onto my initial contact, and I would have to serve a back-to-back tour right after my duty was fulfilled in Italy.

On December 28, 1982, another message come through the communication station from D.C. regarding my NATO assignment. A background investigation, psychological examination, an additional set of fingerprints, and dental records were mandatory requests that had to be performed before my transfer.

Naval Intelligence Service (NIS) conducted its background investigation on me by showing up in my hometown of Peru. NIS scoured my old Polish neighborhood and asked the neighbors questions about my character, childhood, and behavior. I found out about this information when my mother called me. She was upset wondered what was going on with me.

"There are men in suits walking around the neighborhood asking questions about you. Lucille came over and told me that these agents were asking her questions too. She was wondering if you were in any kind of trouble. What's going on?" my mother pleaded.

"Do not worry, Ma. I was granted a position in NATO that's going to change my security clearance status with the service." I explained to her.

"NATO?"

"Yeah, NATO, you know Northern Atlantic Treaty Organization."

"Well, I don't know, but anyway, what kind of changes are you talking about?"

"My security clearance requires a higher level than what my current clearance is," I vaguely replied.

"But you already have a top secret clearance, and I thought you were going to be stationed in San Diego until you got out of the Navy. I don't quite understand all of this," she blankly expressed.

"Everything is fine; I will explain later. Just let Lucille and the other neighbors know that I am NOT in any kind of trouble." I reassured her.

I passed all of my background checks: physical, mental, and background investigations. Cosmic Atomic Top Secret Clearance was granted, whatever that meant. I was on my way to begin a new adventure but not before I had a performance evaluation completed.

A performance evaluation was mandatory before anyone leaves her or his duty station. My period of performance covered from February 10, 1982 to February 16, 1983.

"Seaman Turczyn is an efficient watch stander who strives for perfection in all areas assigned. She is always respectful towards her co-workers and willingly follows orders, always attempting to carry them out with the utmost speed and accuracy while exhibiting an excellent example for all to follow. Seaman Turczyn continually maintains an impressive appearance in both military and civilian attire. Her congenial nature, coupled with her most favorable attitude, has enabled her to contribute to the high morale within her watch section. Her ability to interact within the integrated workforce of this command is indicative of her support of the Navy's Equal Opportunity Program. Recently advanced to E-3, Seaman Turczyn is highly recommended for retention in the naval service. The occasion for this evaluation is due to Seaman Turczyn's transfer on 16

February 1983."

Leaving San Diego was difficult for me. The ocean side town was my first duty station, and I had grown quite attached to it. The part that hurt the most was saying good-bye.

The civilian and military personnel I met while stationed in San Diego taught me many lessons. A few outstanding individuals: Beth, Kim, Bob, and Peggy taught me the rewards of friendship. We had each other's backs. And, I met one outstanding marine: Allen Boettcher.

I met Al one glorious day when I was walking across the plaza at Ford Hall. Strolling along with nothing but carefree feelings taking over my body, I took my time walking to my room. The San Diego sun begged me to take off my naval cap to let it shine upon my face. And I did, even though it was against the naval uniform code. As the sun offered its warmth, I heard a marine whistle from the 3rd floor. Instantly, I knew it was for me. I looked up as the sun squeezed its brightness into my eyes. Squinting, a man came into focus. He stole my heart while I took his.

Al didn't have one ounce of body fat on him. A tall frame bent over to rest his elbows on the iron railing. A cigarette dangled between his massive hands. I took in every moment of this man's glaring confidence. His brave tenacity ignited a wild passion deep inside my soul. Immediately, I wanted this marine. I wanted to be standing in front of him and close enough to feel his heartbeat against my chest and to explore that daring face with my eager fingertips. My body was drawn to him like a magnet until I stood face to face with this new found stranger; a fresh love.

Two sets of green eyes starred back at each other and life was never the same for me.

I loved him, and he loved me. Our romance was filled with passionate days and nights riding his motorcycle every chance we got. As we sped through "our San Diego," I clung to him as my arms hugged his torso from behind. I could feel his warm flesh through the thin white T-shirt he always wore, as I pressed my chest up against him.

Al's motorcycle took off like a rocket every time we whizzed on the freeways, darting in and out between the cars, and racing to get to our favorite place; the beach.

Al was the first man I ever felt safe with. In his presence, I always felt that no harm would ever touch me again as long as Al was by my side. His love and dedication to God and country far superseded anyone else's in the military. Dedication was a uniform he never took off for his fellow marines. It ran deep within his American veins with such a fierce loyalty. I have never admired another man in all of my life as much as I admired Al.

Sadly though, I didn't know how to love myself, so my loving him was not fair or just. He deserved better. Al showed me that a man could love a woman without his fists. I threw it all away because worthlessness captured any feelings as our love began to grow. I didn't know how to take the unconditional love he offered me and wrap it around myself forever like ribbons on a gift. I broke his heart and caused him pain all because my abusive past conquered what was good and just in me. My diseased blood thirsted for more of Al's love, but I denied the love I deserved the most.

So my lessons continued, as I left San Diego. Many people lied to me because it was the answer for everything. They did it without remorse and with a sweet smile spread across their faces. I was so young and gullible and smiled right back at them, believing every tale of fallacy that spilled from their forked tongues. Humiliation exposed itself all over me, as I walked down the corridors of Balboa Hospital, bathed in my own urine.

I learned to become a master of deception to hide my physical and emotional pain just to survive. As the journey of life unfolded before me, I discovered that stuffing the pain, whether it was emotional or physical, came too easy for me. Many, many attempts were made to find the "hidden pain" and nurture its existence. However, it was another part of my self-survival technique that automatically engaged, so I could live.

But I have never forgotten my marine.

CHAPTER SEVENTEEN

I EXCHANGED SAN Diego and the Pacific Ocean for Naples, Italy and the Mediterranean Sea. The flight to Italy left on March 23, 1983 from Philadelphia. My parents and I drove from Illinois to Pennsylvania, so we could spend some time together before my overseas departure. Our relationship was still strained, but not like it was when I lived under their roof. Maybe they were a little proud of me, and the medical stresses were not present in their lives any more.

However, in my junior year of high school, my mother had to have a total hysterectomy, and she had half of her lung removed due to histoplasmosis; an infection caused by breathing in spores of a fungus from bird and/or bat droppings. My mother never gave up. She always pushed forward in life.

Before we left for Philadelphia, some family members stopped by our house to say their farewells. My father's side of the family is Polish, and my mother's side is Polish and Irish.

Bernard and Esther were my grandparents, mom's mother and father. They dropped by our home the day before we were leaving for Philadelphia. My father's mother, Marie, the grandmother who gave me the gifts of laughter and dreams, was not there. Sadly, she passed away. Cigarette smoking and other contributory health conditions took her life. Her husband Flex was still alive, but he lived in a nursing home in the nearby town of Spring Valley.

Both sets of grandparents were so different but equally loved by me.

When Bernard and Esther arrived at our home, my grandfather brought his polished, wooden cane. He wore his usual snappy green jacket, black dress pants, a white long sleeved shirt, and his dangling silver bolero tie.

My grandmother followed behind, matching Bernard's dressy attire with black dress pants, a lily white ruffled blouse, and black leather shoes with small heels. A strand of pearls hung around her neck, as they slowly made their distinguished arrival up the back porch steps.

The name alone, Esther Liss, speaks only of class. Esther's habits, mannerisms, and philosophies were so diverse from my other grandmother, Marie. But together, they added an essential balance to my life.

One step into her immaculate green and white kitchen was like stepping into a spring day after a rain shower. The fragrance of fresh tulips invaded my nostrils and tickled my nose. It seemed that the sun was the only source of light emulating from this holy ground. The clean, fresh, starchy white curtains rode the winds coming in from kitchen windows, adding to the freshness of nature's natural odor.

Esther was petite and possessed sharp Irish facial features. Her snowy, white hair accented her cornflower blue eyes. Grandmother's stylish outfits came only from Ireland, or so I wanted to believe. However, it was her kind smile that I admired about this fine lady.

When my sister and I were not staying at Marie's house, we were at Esther's. Both grandmothers took turns watching us while my mother was sick, and Dad was trying to keep us out of bankruptcy.

Esther introduced us to the *Lawrence Welk Show.* Stretched out on the living room floor on our stomachs, chins resting in the palm of our hands, Janie and me watched Sissy and Bobby dance before the orchestra. The smoothness of their movements as they glided into each other's arms while twirling with ease across the glass floor brought fantasies of romantic dances I could hardly wait for my feet to explore.

Grandmother Esther did not allow us to watch too much TV programs like Marie did. If nature or educational programs were not among the TV listings, the TV was not among the living. Her ancient phonograph came back to life with the wave of Hammerstein's wand commanding breath into the strings of the London Promenade Orchestra. Themes from *Doctor Zhivago*, *Lawrence of Arabia*, Tchaikovsky's *Swan Lake*, and *Sleeping Beauty* are still alive in my collection of musical memories.

The love of music was not all we shared. I was born on her birthday, May 28th, a day dear to my heart. She gave me the gifts of appreciation for nature, dance, and the fine arts.

Since birth, I was always Bernard's little princess. He always said that I was his little movie star who far outshined anyone on the screen today.

As Grandfather sat down in the living room chair, he patted the armrest for me to take a seat. I loved the attention that he showered on me dearly. When I ran away as a kid, I always went to their house in LaSalle. My grandfather was upset about my departure to Italy.

Grandmother kept saying, "Now Dad (she called grandfather dad), she will be just fine."

Bernard disagreed, not because of me, but the uncertain times we lived in.

Ronald Reagan was my commander in chief at the time. I was getting stationed overseas. "Star Wars" was at the height of its expansion and nuclear warheads were being shipped all over the world.

Grandfather was concerned about my safety, and he had every right to be.

When the time came for my grandparents to depart, Grandfather solemnly swore to me, "You will never see me again. I shall die before you return."

Goose bumps covered my entire body, as I turned to him and sternly protested. Shoving my head into his massive chest, I said, "Oh, grandpa stop, it. Stop it right now!"

Unfortunately, my grandfather's prophecy came true. That visit was the last time I ever saw him.

These are the military sacrifices our men and women do for the country that we love so dearly.

Saying good-bye to my new nephew Matthew, brother-in-law Gary, and most of all, my sister Janie, felt like the wind was getting sucked out from my lungs. There was not enough air on this earth to obtain a proper breath. I could not get on the plane and fly to Illinois in a matter of hours because an entire ocean separated us.

Three years older than me, my sister was my best friend. Her birthday is the day after mine; May 29th. We used to celebrate our birthdays together, always. Janie was with me throughout all of my childhood heartaches and the frightening times when Mom was so sick, and we were so afraid. But we never spoke of our heartaches or the abuse we endured while it was happening. Why didn't we ever speak of the pain? It was almost as if we were living in fog.

One time, I skipped etymology class, and she hid my absentee slip that arrived from Gordy Rogers, the principal of LaSalle-Peru

High School. She knew if dad found out I would be coming home to a beating, for sure.

Janie heard Marie on the phone one day when we were just kids saying, "You know their mother isn't going to live. These kids are going to be orphans. God, the secrets that we kept buried.

I said my good-byes, and I left my sister crying outside standing in our front yard. I felt like I was abandoning her with the memories alone to face: our secrets. But she had a new family now. As she stood next to our house, she lifted her arm to wave, while holding my nephew, Matthew. He waved good-bye, too.

CHAPTER EIGHTEEN

WE ARRIVED IN Philadelphia, checked into a hotel, and had a quiet dinner. Ma and dad made sure I had enough money. They sewed some money into the inside of the hem of my coal, black navy coat. The Polish!

And Esther made a small white rectangular pouch with a zipper that fit nicely inside my brassiere. Money was placed inside that, too. To this day, I still have that little, white homemade pouch.

My parents gave me advice and told me to call them as soon as I arrived in Naples.

The next day, we made our way to the airport. Arrow Air was the name of the airplane carrier that transported me to a mystical, yet exciting foreign country. My first military aircraft was otherwise known as a MAC-flight.

When I began to think about how far away I was actually going to be from home, panic spread throughout my body. Thank God for ignorance!

I stood on that airfield not wanting to go beyond the chain-linked fence. Then, I saw Federal Marshals escort prisoners onto the same plane I was to board.

The prisoners' arms and legs were shackled and their dirty hair hung down to their shoulders. These were deserters of the armed forces and were being escorted back to their duty stations for trial, according to gossip I heard.

Why would the government spend all that money transporting these guys back to a foreign country when they could have been tried right here in the states? The prisoners were government property at that point. How odd I thought to myself.

Hastily hugging ma and dad for one last time, I stuffed the feelings of terror that rose in my fear and denial room, and then marched beyond the chain-linked fence. I kept on waving at my parents until my mother buried her face into dad's chest. At least, they had each other to hold onto.

The flight was crowded and stuffy. All four branches of the military were represented on this flight: army, navy, air force, marines, and the officers and enlisted. There were also civilian personnel. Every seat on the plane was occupied. The seats were even closer than the commercial airliners if you can even imagine that: tight and snug.

Our in-flight meals consisted of cardboard sandwiches complimented with a mouthful of fruit juice from a tiny plastic container.

The pregnant woman sitting next to me asked for seconds and sometimes thirds of our tasteless food. She kept reminding the flight attendant with a pat to her swollen belly that she was eating for two.

I could barely ingest the food in this cattle car with wings. Staring out the tiny window scared me out of my mind. Yet, I was excited with anticipation about my next adventure.

Unknown to me, the plane was not going directly Italy. Our first stop was Roda, Spain to drop off some military personnel and pick some others up. While the plane refueled, we got off to stretch our legs and get some air. Taking off on time was not the plan. The plane had some mechanical problems. Two hours later, we boarded the plane again and were off to Sicily; another destination I did not know was included in our flight plan.

The same routine occurred in Sicily as in Roda minus the mechanical problems.

Finally, we landed in Naples, Italy, and my heart pounded like a jackhammer, yet I was too tired to even articulate one word. As she walked down the aisle, a flight attendant informed us that we were in Naples and to get off the plane.

After seventeen hours, I was ready for a shower and clean air. I stunk. However, what awaited my eager senses was far from fresh.

As I cautiously disembarked, a disgusting odor flew up my nostrils. I held back the vomit inching up the middle of my throat. I grabbed a tissue from my coat pocket and wrapped it around my mouth. The smell reminded me of rotten eggs. Finding my way through the dinky terminal, I kept the tissue close to my face.

Military personnel from different branches stood in the terminal holding up signs with names on them. These people were sponsors for the new incoming military personnel and escorted them back to the appropriate bases.

Desperately, I scanned the crowd for my name, but unfortunately for me, TURCZYN in large, black block letters, did not appear on anyone's white cardboard sign. Retrieving my luggage, I stood there dumbfound as anxiety washed all over me.

I was petrified. Not knowing where I was going or what was outside that terminal door was overwhelming. Standing with my carpet printed suitcase and sea bag, I watched as everyone left with a sponsor.

I was the only one left in the terminal. Sitting down on a nearby wooden bench, I waited. For what, I didn't know.

Thirty minutes later, a woman in a naval uniform popped her head around the corner and said, "Didn't anybody pick you up?"

"No," I replied too loudly, while choking back tears and trying to remain calm. But my anxiety was winning.

"Where are you going to be stationed at? At the naval base or NATO?" she questioned me.

"NATO," I replied.

"Why don't you come with us? We're going over there, too."

A sigh of relief shivered throughout my body, as I quickly stood up and followed her to the car. Luckily for me, she actually was a member of the U.S. Armed Forces working for the Department of Defense and not someone who was there to harm Americans. All I was concerned about was getting into the car, reporting to my duty station, and wondering what that God-awful smell was! I did not even think about the security risks or danger.

"Brownie, my name is Brownie," she stated as she offered me her hand.

She was a beautiful black woman with skin that only women in a magazine would own: soft, clear, and creamy.

"What's that horrible smell?"

She threw her head back and roared with laughter.

"*Solfatara*!"

"*Solfatara.* What's that?" I asked her while covering my nose with the tissue.

"Get used to it. It's the gases from the volcanoes around here.

The monstrous Mt. Vesuvius lives here and that smell never goes away," she chuckled as we tried to squeeze into one of the smallest vehicles I had ever seen.

CHAPTER NINETEEN

I THOUGHT TO myself, Volcanoes? Volcanoes were in Hawaii, not Italy.

I sat back and took in all of the scenery and wondered what a volcano was doing in Italy. My knowledge of geography and topography was limited at this point in my life. However, the education train soon began to accelerate once I set foot on foreign ground.

The highways were like speedways, and the Italians were the racecar drivers. My eyes could not take in all of the near misses. I squeezed them shut and prayed for a safe arrival at the military base. When I did open them, flashes of bright colors blurred past our car. Feeling an acidy liquid creep its way up my throat, I was going to be sick. The car veered off the speedway and onto the exit ramp. Suddenly, we came to a stop.

Cars! They were everywhere. This traffic jam was massive. Every driver fought for every inch of the road while cars collided into us. People yelled in Italian and waved their fists. It felt like I was sitting in a bumper car at an amusement park and my go pedal was stuck.

"What's going on?" I asked Brownie.

"Just up ahead is the shortest, yet infamous alley in all of Naples. It's called *Squeeze Alley.*

Quickly, I learned why they called it *Squeeze Alley.* All these cars and trucks were trying to squeeze through a narrow passage way known as the neck of the alley that led into various streets. A lot of strategic maneuvering was involved in to squeeze your car through the alleyway. Some of the Italians got out of their cars and played cards on the hoods of their automobiles while the ignition was on. Puffing away on their long cigarettes, a few shared the newspaper, while we waited for our turn to enter the narrow passage.

Once we got into the skinny street, the traffic crept along. One fellow drove onto the sidewalk, not because he was impatient. It was a strategic move as if driving on sidewalks were normal. I kept that information in my memory bank for future use when I had to maneuver throughout the roadways of Naples.

Brownie told me to get use to the chaotic driving and Squeeze Alley because there were only two ways to get into the NATO base.

We ended up going to the navy base first before my duty station. As we pulled up to the base, a marine stood at the gate and waved our car ahead. My fatigue was winning the battle in my head. As I slowly got out of the car, everything hurt: my legs, arms, eyeballs, butt, and stomach. I had been up for over twenty-four hours.

We arrived at our first stop, the Naval Air Base when Brownie shouted, "Let's get a cappuccino!"

This was the first time that I had tasted a cappuccino.

Brownie instructed me to put spoonful after spoonful of sugar into the white froth. I must have not put enough sugar in the petite cup because my taste buds hollered, "Bitterness!" Then, my stomach began to cramp.

"Lie down! I want to fall onto a soft bed!" I was extremely fatigued and could not keep my eyes open a minute longer.

Brownie kept on encouraging me to stay up because of the time difference. She promised me I would sleep that night. Frankly, I was not concerned about the night but more with sinking into unconsciousness. Finally, we left the naval base and headed towards the NATO base.

The two bases were only a few miles apart. On the way to NATO, I noticed an elderly, heavyset woman sitting on a crumbling stone wall. She had bleached blonde hair, red ruby lips, and too much frosty blue eye shadow on her heavy eyelids. She kept pushing up the red spaghetti straps on her sleeveless summer top; the small top barely covered her monstrous breasts. Accompanying her heavy make-up were small streaks of dirt covering her entire body. She used a white handkerchief to wipe the sweat from her brow and the moisture inside her deep cleavage.

Everyone called her "Humpty Dumpty" because she spent so much time sitting on top of that crumbling wall. Old stones were stacked on top of each other, but it wasn't a high barrier. Actually, it looked quite comfortable. The wall only required a short leap from where she was sitting to the sidewalk. She was part of the Italian scenery. However, I felt nothing but sorrow for this old woman whose daily pain led her to the wall for reasons only she knew.

Allied Forces Southern Europe (AFSOUTH) was an impressive base. As we approached the NATO entrance, several men guarded the gates with machine guns, otherwise known as the Carabinieri. Their uniforms were midnight blue with red and white trim, and their caps were tightly secured with a black chinstrap. Their uniforms looked just as gallant as the men who wore them. Yet, I feared their presence.

Brownie warned me that as soon as I received my Italian driver's license to be mindful of the Carabinieri.

"They carry white sticks with large red circles attached to the tops. The Americans call it the lollipop wand. If the Carabinieri ever waves it at you, you need to pull over immediately to the side of the road. If you don't pull over, they'll shoot your tires right off. Also, make sure your license and registration are quickly available!"

I asked Brownie, "How do you know if they are waving the wand at you with so many cars around?"

"If there's ever a doubt in your mind, pull over!" she shouted.

I had that doubt one time, and I pulled over, along with ten other vehicles.

We waited until an unfortunate person was selected to have the lollipop placed on the hood of their car. Then, we were waved away as the Carabinieri got on with their interrogation.

However, no one was in a hurry then. We looked in our rear view mirrors while cautiously inching our vehicles back onto the roadway, afraid to move too fast, just in case we were not excused yet.

As we drove onto the NATO base, I was astonished by all of the different types of uniforms. I never realized that there could be so many colorful pieces of clothing and stylish outfits. This base might have been easily mistaken for a military fashion show instead of an allied forces base.

Britain, France, Turkey, Greece, Italy, and the Unites States occupied this base. All the military branches within each country were represented: navy, air force, army, and the marines. I could not distinguish the British Navy from the British Air Force or a French officer from a French enlistee.

As far as saluting to the NATO personnel, I raised my right

hand over my brow to everyone that walked by me wearing foreign attire for fear of being disrespectful. Many times I just avoided the unknown uniform by going in the other direction or bending down to tie my shoe, until I learned the proper attire and ranks of my foreign comrades.

After partially checking in at the personnel department, I was taken to Pozzuoli: the United States military barracks via taxi. I said good-bye to Brownie and profusely thanked her for letting me join her caravan instead of waiting at the Naples airport for the no show sponsor. If I saw her today, I would thank her one more time.

The ride to the barracks in Pozzuoli was twenty minutes long and my education continued. A taxi-driver from the base took me to my new home. The winding road led up to an unknown destination. This moment was the first time I had ever witnessed extreme poverty and captivating beauty all at the same time.

My curious ears and eyes were wide open, as I absorbed all the surrounding foreign sounds and the mountainous landscapes. A herd of sheep in the narrow road halted our climb for several minutes. Such a foreign place for me, and yet I embraced this world, as the sheep slowly trotted by our taxi. A few of them stopped and looked right at me. I stared back into their eyes. Soaking in the experience and chuckling to myself at these dirty sheep, I swore some of them smiled at me. They were so close to the taxi I could reach out and touch their wooly fur. My eager hands wanted to sink into their fleece, but I decided against that spontaneous gesture.

With the herd behind us, finally we continued our ascension.

Where was I going to live? The anticipation was maddening. To my surprise, the barracks were not on the NATO base. My new environment was invigorating and diverse, but I could not let my adventurous spirit run free just yet. A chilling grip surrounded my heart and kept it captured.

The driver made a sharp left turn and drove down a steep hill into an underground parking garage. It felt like I was on a roller coaster getting ready to take the plunge down the first dive on the track. The driveway wasn't in view. Where were we going? Down into the sea!

Suddenly, I saw it. The barracks looked like a high rise nestled in the hillside, tucked away from the public's view, hidden among nature's serenity.

Before the taxi driver pulled away, he told me that on the top of the hill there was a bus service to transport the military personnel back and forth to the bases. He gave me the schedule and sped off.

I found my way up to the main floor and handed my orders to the petty officer sitting behind the desk.

Appearing to be unconcerned, he said, "All of the rooms are occupied. You will have stay at a hotel across from the naval base."

Collapsing on my bags, I could not believe the matter of fact words he said. Then, he walked away.

What did he mean no rooms here? I'm a military person! You know, the same as you! I belong here with you.

He gave me a voucher to pay for my unlimited time at the American Hotel and left me aghast.

I spotted a chair in the lobby and sank into it, exhausted. I was too tired to care anymore. Playing human Monopoly wasn't what I had planned to do today. Unfortunately, I picked up the card instructing me to go to home, and of course, I did not collect my two hundred dollars!

Gathering every ounce of strength, I threw the sea bag over my shoulder and grabbed a hold of my suitcase's strap and attacked the steep hill. Huffing my way up to the top, I finally made it. I waited for the bus to take me back to the first base.

Finally, it arrived two hours later. As fatigue stuck to me like a wet blanket and deliriousness swarmed inside my head, I checked into the hotel. Of course, I did not speak Italian. Once I got through the language barrier, my sea bag, suitcase, and weary body climbed a flight of stairs, and I found the room. Lying down on the twin bed with all of my clothes on, I immediately gave into the darkness.

CHAPTER TWENTY

WHILE TRYING TO fend off the fatigue that still plagued my body, I woke up the next morning confused. It felt like someone had poured glue into my mouth, as I spat into the sink. After a steamy, hot shower, and brushing my teeth several times, I put on a fresh uniform. Grabbing my cover, purse, and paperwork, I dashed downstairs and hailed a taxi to the NATO base.

My mother made sure that I had some lire in my pocket before I left home. I still did not know how to calculate lire to the dollar, so I gave the taxi driver some lire and in my weak Italian, said, "Bene?" I probably gave him double the amount.

After checking in at the NATO base, I didn't have to report to duty until after a week-long class called *Culture Shock* was completed.

Culture Shock prepared the new military and civilian personnel for the Italian culture and customs. There were twenty people in the class. We were all in a state of confusion and tiredness. The class consisted of military and civilian personnel, and dependents. A dependent can be a spouse or a child of the service man or woman, or civilian personnel. In my class, there were a few familiar faces from the plane ride over to Italy.

The instructor was an enlisted Navy Petty Officer First Class. He was extremely enthusiastic about Italy and its customs. It showed through his teaching style and facial expressions. His wife just happened to be Italian.

This class taught us about the dangers and the rules of living overseas as Americans working for the Department of Defense. We were rationed specific items and had to use a ration card to purchase them. Cigarettes, liquor, and fuel were on the list. In addition, Europe was based on the metric system, so the gasoline was allotted in liters. He advised us about which gas stations would take the ration cards and the gas stations to stay away from. Also, he warned the class about the black market and what could happen if we were caught dealing in it. After hearing about the punishment and jail sentence, I did not know why anyone would even want to risk getting locked up in a foreign country and losing his or her rank. Though, greed had a powerful hold on many people in Naples.

The instructor encouraged the class not to wear our uniforms while traveling back and forth to work. Only wear your uniform at work, he advised. Do not be seen in your uniform outside of the base at all. NATO personnel were highly recommended to never wear their uniforms to work. A sparkling, white navy uniform brought too much attention to kidnappers. If military personnel were caught wearing their uniforms to work, they would be written up and punished.

Finally, I got to hear about the cause of that awful stench! Unfortunately, Brownie was right. The smell of rotten eggs was due to the volcanoes around the southern tip of Italy: Olympian Etna, Stromboli, Mount Epomeo, and Mount Vesuvius. Mt. Vesuvius affected Naples the most because of the lava-lake of solfatara. The rotten odor came from that surrounding region.

I turned to the person next to me in class and said, "I do believe that the Navy left that portion out of the welcome to Italy brochure."

Stationed in San Diego, I felt the tremors from a few minor earthquakes. When they struck, it felt like my equilibrium was off. My body swayed in unison with the communication station. But the earthquakes or small tremors only lasted a few seconds. However, in Naples, there would be no question in anyone's mind when an earthquake struck. The instructor told us that we would be picking ourselves up off the ground, getting in our cars, and fleeing the area because the aftershocks were just as damaging as the earthquakes.

In addition, I learned that the Neapolitans were intensely superstitious. They carried good luck charms around with them. St. Christopher and St. Peter medals dangled around their necks and wrists to ward off evil spirits. Whenever a funeral procession passed by them in the streets, they cast their eyes and bodies away, and quickly blessed themselves. The Italians considered it bad luck if death looked upon Neapolitans because then, death would come to them.

Also, the instructor advised us to never knock on car windows that had newspaper plastered all over the insides. In the square where Humpty Dumpy sold her services, it always looked like a used car lot around lunchtime. The lot was part of the Italian culture and came to life briefly in the afternoons, and then, turned back into the same vacant lot by dusk. The newspapers were used for privacy; whereas, the cars functioned as the romantic shelter for sexual urges that had to be met immediately.

I could not believe it! People making love right in the middle of the public square? The newspaper surrounding the lovers created a paper fort, so their endearments were displayed in a private fashion among the daily headlines. This arrangement was not my idea of romance, but I always had to remind myself that this was not my country.

Remembering my high school days, which were only a year ago, I giggled. The old, country road served our purpose for exchanging passionate kisses and the darkness was our paper fort. So, are we really that different even though we grew up in different countries? Absolutely not!

The last day of class was on a Friday. Now, we were ready to try out our new Italian education out in the city. With all the Italian culture and customs crammed into our Americanized heads, we were eager to apply what we learned.

We were all set free in Pozzuoli and ready for the culture challenge. Personally, I believe that anyone who has never been out of the United States should do so for two reasons: gratitude and education.

Some of the things I took for granted were language, hot water, ice cubes, heat, security, the stable ground beneath my feet, washing machines and dryers, restrooms, sanitation, telephones, electricity, and time schedules. And when you call a plumber, the service person will be there the same day, not three months later.

CHAPTER TWENTY-ONE

WORKING FOR NORTHERN Atlantic Treaty Organization (NATO) Allied Forces Southern Europe was one of the most important positions I ever held. A World War II tunnel was its place of operation. To get to my workstation, I had to pass several security checks: the entrance into base, tunnel, and then several codes to open the largest cast iron door I had ever seen.

Many times throughout the year, NATO participated in worldwide exercises (war games) requiring some of us to go off base into some never never land. Where, I still cannot say to this day. I traveled to different locations, other than the NATO base, and worked several miles underground. During these long hours of operation, I excelled rapidly in the job.

In March of 1984, I received a certificate of achievement for the Operation Dense Corp. This was written on it: "This certificate is presented to RMSN Debra J. Turczyn for your outstanding duty performance during a NATO exercise. Your versatility and dedication contributed significantly to the success of this critical exercise. J. L. Pedersen, Lt. Colonel, USAF-Commander."

In addition, I also received another evaluation from the period of March 23, 1983 to January 31, 1984. While in the Navy, this one was the highest rating I had ever received.

The Navy works on a 1.0 to a 4.0 evaluation system with 4.0 being the highest:

Reliability 4.0

Personal Behavior 4.0

Human Relations including Equal Opportunity 4.0

Military Knowledge/Performance 3.8
Rating Knowledge/Performance 3.8
Initiative 3.8
Military Bearing 3.6
Overall Rating 3.8

The evaluation continued, "RMSN Turczyn is a respected and loyal member of the communication operations squadron staff message center. An excellent performer, Seaman Turczyn has shown her ability to work well either independently or with a team on any given task, regardless of how major or minor it may be. During stressful situations, such as major exercises, she again demonstrates her flexibility and knowledge of NATO communications, which contributes to their success.

Following commands without question and constantly offering assistance where it is needed in order to help others, she further demonstrates her value to this communications facility and the U.S. Navy respectfully. RMSN Turczyn has completed military and professional requirements for Radioman 3rd Class and 2nd Class and has passed the military leadership examination for Petty Officer Third Class. Showing a determination for self-improvement, RMSN Turczyn actively supports the Equal Opportunity Program, as is demonstrated not only with member of the U.S. Forces but also with all members of the NATO community. RMSN Turczyn should be considered highly recommended for promotion and retention in the United States Navy." LCDR K.M. Goldstein, OIC

What can I say? I loved the Navy!

CHAPTER TWENTY-TWO

AS MUCH AS I enjoyed my job, immersing myself in the Italian culture, I still was not feeling well. My health began to decline, once again. On February 15, 1984, I presented myself at sick call because for the last couple of months, I started to experience symptoms I could not comprehend.

For no apparent reason, I woke up in the middle of the night with my pajamas completely soaked with sweat. My hair was so wet it was like I had just washed it in the sink. Several sleepless nights coupled with these immense hot flashes that popped up all the time, I thought I was going nuts. Severe heart palpations led me to believe I had a heart condition.

Hot flashes were the words I used to describe my symptoms unaware there really were such symptoms (remember, I was twenty-one years old and extremely naïve about my reproductive system.)

Placing a fan in front of my face along with a bowl of ice, I prayed for the heat penetrating from my body and face to subside. Sometimes, only one side of my face and ear got just as red as a clown's nose, while the other side remained pale. Feeling like I had an internal furnace that switched on whenever it wanted, I sought out anything cold to a slap on my face, ears, and back.

I brought changes of clothes to work because the profuse sweating was ruining my uniforms. The armpit areas were canary yellow.

The skin on my hands and elbows became dry and old while my heart raced on. It was the only part of my body that felt like it was running a marathon.

What happened next was completely foreign: depression. It followed me everywhere. No matter what challenges I had to face until this point in my life, I never felt such sadness under any circumstances. A smile was my daily attire, as I kept on pushing away any obstacle I encountered.

The explanation for this depleted state was unknown to me at the time. Before these symptoms started to appear in my body, I was boating to the Isle of Capri, dancing in the clubs in Rome, exploring the ruins in Pompeii, eating pizza at Due Palma, and hanging out with the people I worked with on base.

I became really close friends with Tim Gunderman, We worked those atrocious hours in the tunnel: 7:00 AM to 7:00 PM for two days and then 7:00 PM to 7:00 AM for an additional two days. He played his guitar and composed songs for me. Tim was my "go to man" and I enjoyed every second I spent with him. I adored and loved him and trusted him whole heartedly.

So back to the hospital I went. This time the roaring hot flashes consumed me. Sweat ran down my face and back, and the naval doctor saw it. I was grateful that the doctor saw these symptoms: red face, sweat coming out of every pore, and my heart racing. It proved to the doctor that this medical condition was not in my head. The evidence made itself known! The doctor felt my slippery, soaked back and forehead and sent me down to the GYN office.

A follicle stimulating hormone (FSH) test was performed. However, the doctor said that test results were fine.

"Fine! Fine for whom for you? I want to feel normal again!" I shouted at him.

How could I be fine when these symptoms were obviously present? Physical signs of something that was medically wrong, I thought.

I was given Compazine and sent back to work. This drug is for the severe nausea, vomiting, and anxiety. Disgusted and exhausted from the runaround, I left the hospital in Naples and worked my twelve-hour shift.

CHAPTER TWENTY-THREE

May 29, 1984

MY FELLOW MANKIND

I feel like I am out here alone in a sea of contempt screaming for help.
Why can't you hear my obvious cries with every sound I speak and see my hesitation in every move I take?
The waves of cruelty are crashing down upon my sunburned shoulders as I try to stay afloat.
They are plunging deeper and deeper into the depths of hopelessness drowning out my desperate pleas.
I am choking.
I am grasping for an out reached hand to set me free.
I lay defenseless among the predators as they feed their savage hunger ripping through my skin, only to find that the humans had reached my innards first.
Gradually, I emerge to the calm surface as my hollow cadaver surrenders to mankind.
I can feel no pain.
I have never felt the love.

***

I awoke feeling unbalanced and ill again, but something was different inside of me. Suffering since February with these crazy symptoms, a plague of utter despair conquered my inner strength. It was as if the devil stuffed himself inside of me and burned my brain. Not again, please God, not again. Why isn't anyone listening to me? I felt nauseous and completely off balance. As the days grew old, I began to die.

My suffering body and dehydrated mind surrendered to the consistent absence of hormones and the ever so present depression. How much more obvious did my condition have to get? The deterioration of my mind and the physical characteristics clearly screamed for rejuvenation and hormonal nourishment.

Lying in bed became my refuge. I could not ignore the hot flashes burning inside of me anymore. Even after I quenched them with several cold showers, the fire continued to consume my flesh. Nothing stopped the flames.

My shift at the NATO base started at 7:00 PM and ended at 7:00 AM. At 6:00 PM, I pressed my dungarees as sweat dripped from my forehead and onto the ironing board. The starch filled creases would have passed the scrutiny of any detailed inspecting officer. Placing freshly ironed clothes on a hanger, I put on a T-shirt, shorts, tennis shoes, walked onto the balcony, and looked into the horizon.

For the first time in my life, I could not see past the setting sun. As a single tear rolled down the side of my face, I began to shake. Grabbing my brown paper sack, I got into my Volkswagen and never looked back.

The ride into Naples was a blank canvas. I felt numb. Nothing was left inside of me. I drove to the hospital parking lot because eventually someone would find me during the night. The military would put me in a body bag and send me home.

Lost in a world of obscurity, I found the package in the sack and opened it. Holding the cold razor blade in the palm of my hand, I felt nothing. I picked up the sharp object, grabbed the rearview mirror, and turned it towards my face.

Who was that person in the mirror? I did not recognize the blotchy, distorted reflection, and the pair of exhausted green eyes staring back at me. Watching the last speck of diminishing light flicker out of my eyes, I felt there was no other choice.

Placing the edge of the razor blade into the softness of my wrist, a stream of warm blood appeared and quickly traveled down onto my legs. Today, I can still feel the wet, sticky liquid running over the top of my thighs. As it poured over me, it felt like warm wax. Making quick diagonal and vertical strokes, I dragged the blade up my left forearm until I reached the inside of my elbow. Then, I mutilated the other arm.

I saw flashbacks of beatings, the belt flying in the air, my sister screaming in her bedroom while I covered my ears, the elbow to the gut punches, a sad little girl kneeling on the couch in the rectory crying for her parents to rescue her, and the arguments. The smell of hospital rooms, the absence of my child's touch, the tubes violating my rectum and vagina, the surgeries, pleading and the begging for the pain to stop, and the constant depression occupying my head rushed at me like a tidal wave.

Hearing a pulsating heart inside my head, paralyzing fear latched onto me. A figure dashed by my car as I leaned over to lay my head on the passenger's seat. I tried to clear the flog clouding my actions. Seconds later, I saw him whiz by the car again. Scrunching further down into the seat, my initial reaction was to hide because I was humiliated.

Why was I feeling this way?

What was I doing to myself?

What was I doing sitting in a pool of warm blood trying to end a life that had lost all meaning?

I pushed open the car door and fell to my knees. At that point it was difficult to get my body to do what I wanted. Grabbing the door handle, I yelled at the anonymous man running around in red shorts.

He failed to hear my cries.

"Are you kidding me?" I screamed.

Move, keep moving! Go! Run!

The hospital's entrance was only a short distance away as I half-walked and crawled towards it.

Several people were walking into the hospital, and I yelled at them, too.

Am I dead? Have I reached a place where no one can see or hear me?

I was delirious.

The first face I saw was a navy corpsman standing at hospital's entrance. He was dressed in a white shirt and pants. As he looked at me, I noticed that his face matched the color of his uniform.

Blood and sweat matted my hair. It streaked across my face. My thighs and forearms looked like a botched paint job. Red streaks coated my thighs and splattered red dots pooled around my ankles. Dark, red coagulated blood stuck to my inner forearms, looking like huge thirsty leeches. Tears mixed with blood dripped from my quivering chin as I held out a bloody palm. He refused to take my hand and told me to follow him inside.

Stumbling, I followed him into the hospital corridor. A woman by the name of Brenda escorted me to the emergency room. Then, she besieged me with questions.

"Why, Debbie, why? Why did you do this? Your wrists need to be sutured. When was the last time you had a tetanus shot?" she probed.

Cleansing my wounds, she yelled for help.

Gut wrenching cries came from the depths of my being. Sounds that I never knew existed inside of me came pouring out of my mouth like a wounded animal, as I lay on the emergency room cot.

CHAPTER TWENTY-FOUR

ON MAY 29, 1984 at 9:02 in the evening, I was admitted into the naval hospital. My emergency care and treatment records stated, "Multiple superficial lacerations cut on forearms, alert, oriented, and weepy. No previous episodes. Three sutures were placed in her left wrist and cleansed with betadine. Diagnosis/assessment: suicidal gesture, self-inflected lacerations wrists-Conditions upon release from emergency room-Stable." N. Schlager, MD LT/USNR/AD.

White bandages wrapped my wrists up to my elbows. Oddly enough, I felt some relief, like someone was going to help me through the hot flashes and depression. Somebody had to care enough to know I was experiencing physical and psychological symptoms I had never experienced in my twenty-one years.

"You can make a phone call," said Brenda, the nurse.

"A phone call to where?" I asked her.

"Home-you know-the United States," she carelessly replied.

"My parents?"

"Whoever you want call," she said.

A corpsman escorted me upstairs to the fourth floor and asked me what number I wanted to call.

I was in disbelief. What the hell is going on? Didn't you see what I just did to myself? I don't want to talk to anybody, I screamed inside my head.

Confusion and fear showed on my face, as I hesitantly told the nurse that calling home was not a good idea. My parents would be furious and disappointed in me.

An outstanding sailor, I was advancing at an accelerated rate in my naval career. What happened to me?

I picked up the phone anyway as the corpsman dialed the number I knew by heart. It was early in the morning when my mother answered the phone. She knew right away that something was terribly wrong.

"What happened?" she frantically asked me.

"I slit my wrists," I calmly stated.

Surprisingly, those words slid right out of my mouth. There was no going back, I realized, after saying those words. From now on, my parents would look at me in a different way for the rest of my life.

But would they? Didn't they think I was already somewhat of a challenge to them? I mean they did send me to the priest. Did they ever think that something might be wrong with them?

My world of military accomplishments and personal gains ended as soon as I said those words to her. I could have accomplished many successes in the next twenty years of my life. However, it would never change the way she thought about me ever again.

But it did. In 1998, when I returned home to take care of her before she passed away from stomach cancer. She looked at me like I was a worthy person for the first time.

But for now, I was considered crazy in her mind. Honestly though, how do you lose something that you have never had from your parents anyway? Sadly, one moment in time can change your life forever.

"Don't worry about anything. I hope that the doctors will listen to you. Please don't do this again," my mother sternly said to me.

Just last month, I called my parents and told them something was terribly wrong, again. Something was off, I kept telling them. I just don't feel right. My self-evaluation fell on silent ears with them, too.

The corpsman motioned that I had to hang up the phone and go back to my hospital room.

I said goodbye to my mother, placed the phone back into the, cradle and followed him down the hall.

"Room 412-that's where you'll be staying," he told me and quickly walked away.

There were two other females in room 412. I will never forget that room number. The bed next to the window was unoccupied, so I claimed it.

Later that night, I found out that one of my roommates was bulimic. She threw up her meals into a paper towel and hid the evidence in a garbage can down the hall. The sound of a flushing toilet would have brought too much attention to this woman.

The other woman never spoke. She just held onto her stomach and curled up in a fetal position all day and night.

Across the hall were several OB patients waiting in "The Nest" for the stork to arrive. That is what they called the big room across the hall, "The Nest."

Bewildered about what was going to happen to me, squeezed into my brain. I searched for answers to relieve the symptoms I was feeling, as hot flashes attacked my body again and again.

No one came into the room to see me until the following morning. Nobody checked on me. Nothing. Then, the following day, late into the morning, a team of three doctors came to see me.

Persistently and aggressively they asked, "Why did you do this? Do you know that you're military property and damaging the government?" said one of the doctors.

"You could go to the brig for this!" smirked the other one.

Weeping, I softly said, "Look at me, I can't stop crying, can't sleep, I'm completely exhausted, my skin feels like sandpaper, and I want some relief from these hot flashes and depression. I feel like I am going insane, and why isn't anybody doing anything? Why aren't you listening to me?"

A psychologist by the name of Lt. J. L. Brittain informed me that the Chief of Psychology, Commander Braga, was on temporary assignment and that he was in charge. Lt. Brittain wanted me to know that "he" was the one. "He" was the man. His ego was as big as his baldhead.

Today, if I had to physically describe Lt. Brittain, even though the TV show *The Simpsons* did not exist at that time, he would be Homer's boss, Charles Montgomery Burns-Monty Burns-Mr. Burns. And, he looked exactly like him. He always had a cynical look on his face. Strangely enough, for a psychologist, he lacked communication skills and any bedside manners. His intimidation skills were honed to perfection.

Before he left my room, the doctor told me to have a blood test done at the GYN department. Then he and his team left the room as quickly as they entered.

I sat on my bed and looked out the window. To shut out their incomprehensible responses, I listened to Elton John's *Empty Garden* on my Walkman.

CHAPTER TWENTY-FIVE

May 30, 1984

"THE PATIENT WAS admitted on May 29, 1984. She wants to return to duty and finish her tour. She seems to have done well after she was confronted particularly concerned that she not go back to the United States." J. L. Brittain, PhD.

When I woke up today, depression sat right next to me. But I began to fight back. Since I did not have anyone to speak to about my situation, I gave myself a pep talk and asked God to help me. I begged Him to show me mercy.

Going over the last twenty-four hours in my head, I had to get through this tour of duty and try to find a doctor who could help me. Hang on Debbie! You got this! Get yourself out of this place!

J. L. Brittain informed me that I had to take a multiple-choice test. The questions were weird and repetitive: questions about my sexuality and did I believe in the second coming of Christ. These questions scared and befuddled me. Since I did not understand the concept behind the test or its value, I was not interested in it. Plus, it was very lengthy.

Lt. Brittain handed me a #2 pencil and an answer sheet.

"What's this?" I asked him.

"I need to evaluate you," he said, walking out the door.

He needs to evaluate me with a pencil and a piece of paper.

What's going on here? Nobody's talking to me!

Therefore, like a good little sailor, I answered the questions.

In the afternoon, Lt. Brittain informed me that soon I was going back to full duty.

"What are you going to do to help me? Why am I getting these hot flashes, feeling depressed, and sweating all the time? This isn't normal for me! I want to feel good again and to stop being so weepy!" I replied. "And what about my blood tests? Did you get the results?"

"The test results are negative; everything's fine," he informed me. Then, he turned and left me sitting on the bed with my mouth wide open.

Just like in San Diego, they weren't going to do anything to help me.

"I cannot believe that they are sending me back to full duty," I said to my nameless roommate. "I'm not ready to go back yet; I need some medical attention and most of all, a diagnosis for these symptoms. What if I tried to harm myself again? What's happening here? I need help!"

CHAPTER TWENTY-SIX

May 31, 1984

LT. BRITTAIN ENTERED my room and told me to follow him down the hallway. He had a clipboard in one hand, and his free hand was clenched at his side.

"What's wrong?" I asked him.

"You have to take the written test over again."

Blindly, I followed him. As I trailed behind the doctor, I thought something is not right. Why did I have to take the same test over again? My answers weren't going to be any different than before. Why didn't he hand me a pencil like he did the last time? What was going on?

He rushed into a room and stood by a small table. There was a bed and one window with four panes in it. However, no one could look out of the window because it was placed high in the upper left hand corner of the yellow painted wall. The panes were separated by wood, forming a cross in the middle of the glass. The sun poured through the window and onto the floor before me. A cross shaded the middle of the sunny spot on the tiled floor.

At first, I peeped my head in the doorway, stood in the hallway, and watched Lt. Brittain. I knew this place was a place of no return. Instinctually, my gut knew something was wrong, terribly wrong.

He commanded me to come inside.

I hesitated, grabbed my hospital gown, and twisted the material between my fingers.

"You're changing rooms," he sternly stated.

"I thought I was going back to work," I quietly voiced.

His temper went from 0 to 100. "Get into this room!" he screamed.

As soon as I stepped over the doorway and into the room, my stomach said, "No, not another step. Run!"

My heart was beating as fast as a newborn bunny's. I could feel it pulsating inside my head. The military trained me to obey, and obey I did.

His ferocity did not belie his outward appearance, as he unleashed it like a mad dog. His face turned shades of red as the veins in his neck bulged out, ready to explode. Raising his fist, he pounded the table with such fierce strength that the clipboard bounced with every blow. He picked up the clipboard, slammed it on the table, and screamed, "You're not going to make a fool out of me!"

"What are you talking about?" Shocked, I quietly cried.

"Sit down on the bed now!" he shouted.

Instantaneously, I sat on the bed and placed shaking hands into my lap. Then, I realized there was no test. He had deceived me into coming inside this room.

I kept asking him, "What did I do? Why are you yelling at me?"

His face remained red as rage fled from his eyes and onto me.

"You're not going to make a fool out of me!" he screamed.

He seemed to want me to get mad or angry. Was this his excuse to hit me or to start a physical fight?

Remaining calm, I swallowed fear back down and into the pit of my stomach.

As if on command, two corpsmen came into the room and forced me onto the bed. One of the corpsman plunged a needle into my upper left arm as the other tied me down to the bed with leather straps.

I didn't resist and didn't say a word. I was like silly putty.

"Why are you doing this to me?" I calmly asked going into shock.

I winced from the pain as they tightened the restraints around my wrists. The stitches in my wrist began to tear open. They were tender and sore as the men tied me to the bed. The corpsmen strapped my ankles in leather restraints, as I watched in disbelief.

Four point restraints did not exist in my realm of knowledge. I did not know what these straps were or why they were using them on me.

In shock, I never knew they existed until that defining moment in my life on May 31, 1984.

The unknown injection infected my brain as currents of darkness imprisoned me. Sinking into a well of darkness: sinking, sinking, and sinking; I was dying.

***

The American Dream

Where have I gone?
What place is this I am descending into?
It is so dark.
Why can't I see?
Burning flesh and smoldering hair makes me nauseous as
I try to grip the slippery stone wall.
What awaits my arrival?
Is there no end?
Poker tip flames are piercing the soles of my naked feet.
What am I being crucified for?
My sins have only been to myself.
Where did the laughter of my small child go?
I want to smell fresh daisies in the wind.
My skin is melting on the feverish wall.
Is this the nebbish skin of others left behind that
keeps my traction weak?
I can't see the soaring eagle across the spacious blue sky.
Are there purple mountains?
Will this journey ever end?
Will the torture ever cease?
Why must I slide down the walls of hell in
search of my American Dream?

CHAPTER TWENTY-SEVEN

June 1, 1984

THE SMELL OF fresh daisies did not wake me from the drug-induced sleep. The smell of urine did.

Where was that smell coming from? Where was I?

I felt the cool, damp wetness between my legs.

When did I urinate on myself? Was this urine? It's too sticky.

Saturated in sweat, sticky liquid, and urine, I was unable to move.

What's happened to me?

Fear gripped my head, heart, and soul. It squeezed them like a vice. I was trapped like an animal. A prisoner, but the enemy was one of my own.

Licking my upper lip, I tried to get rid of the mucus draining from my nostrils and dripping into my mouth. My hands and feet were useless. They were betraying me. They, too, were prisoners to the leather restraints. Tears mixed with sweat ran into my mouth, as I kept on licking and licking, while trying to make sense of the last hours.

I yelled for someone, anyone, to help me. No one came.

Struggling to get out of the leather restraints, blood seeped from my wounds, once again. The raw pain stopped me from moving, as I lay perfectly still in urine and stickiness.

Panic. Rising in my chest and throat, it took over my mind and body. I heard and felt the force of the blood and adrenaline racing side by side inside my veins.

Moonlight, the only source of light coming through the window, created the same cross I saw when entering the room. The shadow of the cross.

Somebody help me. Please save me.

Hearing footsteps, I yelled for that person to save me. But saving me was not what he had in mind. Shutting the door, the room turned into midnight minus the stars. I couldn't see anything, but my senses came alive. There was movement in the room; I felt the danger draw near. His breath smelled like an ashtray. A hand pulled up my hospital gown and invaded what was pure and good in me. I tried to scream, but the prick of the needle silenced me. It went deep inside my imprisoned arm. I surrendered, once again, to the current of darkness that captured my soul.

CHAPTER TWENTY-EIGHT

June 2, 1984

A CAUCASIAN BLONDE-haired woman walked into my room. She was corpsman.

"I don't know why they're treating you like an animal. This is disgusting. I don't know what to do," she said while shoving red Jell-O into my mouth.

"I don't understand this treatment or what's going on. I don't want to be a part of this."

As my head slowly turned to face her, she took my blood pressure. Drool and blood seeped from the left side of my mouth. I felt myself floating towards the ceiling.

I'm free. I'm flying away.

"Get a crash cart in here; her blood pressure is dropping. She's going into shock!"

"Stay with me," I mouthed back to the woman.

Footsteps rushed in as they pushed a cart with paddles. Two people gathered around me.

Drifting back into the beckoning darkness, I could not hold onto consciousness. The black hole was welcoming. It was calling me.

While floating overhead, I looked down at my lifeless body. Drifting further and further away from myself, I was still attached to her, to me.

Two military personnel stood around my bedside. They kept injecting needles into my arm.

Darkness-everything went black.

***

I heard a train in the distance, and it was coming fast. I could not cover my ears to block out the noise, but I knew the train would be here to take me home soon.

Watching the ceiling panels rip loose, they landed on my face and legs. Powerless, I watched the debris fall all around me. The room did not stop shaking as squiggly lines raced up the wall, separating it with cracks. The tiles on the wall broke free like they were in a slingshot and fired across the room. The noise was deafening.

Hospital personnel, my fellow service men and women, screamed while they left me behind. Their white uniforms flashed by the doorway, as they ran for their lives.

"Stop, come back! Hey, come and get me! Don't leave me! Untie me!" I was screaming at them while trying to free myself from the leather straps. Tugging and pulling with every bit of strength I had in me, I was trying to survive the inevitable.

Sinking into defeat, I whispered, "Dear God, please don't take me like this."

CHAPTER TWENTY-NINE

"EARTHQUAKE!" PEOPLE SCREAMED. "Run!" "Get the hell out of here!"

It seemed like an eternity before the blonde-haired woman appeared in my room. Pushing away the crash cart, she cleared the debris from the top of the sheets.

"Are you ok?" she frantically asked me. She was losing it.

Paralyzed, I could not talk. My tongue would not function.

Home. I want to go home. Help me. Somebody, please help me.

Staring at the corner of the ceiling panels that remained, I counted the pinholes in the tiles to keep my sanity. I needed to tell myself I was still alive on some level. Counting kept my mental capacities alert, as I thought about the insanity of the entire situation. These people are nuts. She's nuts. How can they think this is normal? What the hell is going on!

The blonde removed the sheet that covered me. She shook it as plaster flew throughout the room. Another corpsman walked in as she threw the dirty sheet on the floor.

While checking my vital signs, they released me from my prison bed. That's what I began to call it: prison. The straps fell away from my wrists and ankles. Was it the same day? I lost track of time. I survived the earthquake?

A male corpsman took me inside the bathroom, but I had already gone in my bed. The bed was my bathroom. Where did the blonde girl go?

Why was he taking me to the bathroom? Why was he closing the door? Why wasn't she taking me to get cleaned up?

I could barely stand as he held me up, and we shuffled to the bathroom. The medication made me dizzy and nauseous.

Trying to lift my head up and keep it stable was not going to happen. It bounced around like a rag doll's as blackness invaded every corner of my eyes. I placed my head on the cold, porcelain sink. Briefly, I glimpsed into the mirror. Who was that girl starring back at me? Greasy brown hair was matted to the sides of my swollen face. Her eyes were vacant.

While he pulled my underpants down, I felt the hard pressure against my rectum as blackness filled my world, again.

I woke up to the sting of another needle as the burning medication seeped into my flesh. Where was I?

Was he the one with the invading footsteps?

When I woke up, clean sheets and a pillow covered my prison bed.

Two corpsmen came in my room and released the restraints. Please God; don't let them tie me up again. Please God, no more, no more.

They left me in two point restraints! My right hand and left ankle were strapped down.

I'll be able to escape. I'll be free soon.

Still in two point restraints, they brought a phone in my room and let me make a phone call. Why did they let me make a phone call? I called Sue, who worked for Environmental Preventive Medical Unit at the naval air base. She was a friend of a friend.

I begged her to come to me and to tell Captain Blanca. Captain Blanca, Captain Blanca's wife, and Sue came up the next day. He knew Captain Braga, who was in charge of the mental health ward, was temporarily away on duty in another country.

The blonde said the doctor wanted me to set myself free in case of any aftershocks or another earthquake. "He wants you to be a good girl."

I have always been a good girl. I am a good sailor.

They left my prison room, but I did not have the courage to escape, or the strength. Like a coward, I felt defenseless and angry for being a good girl.

I hated myself for betraying the girl that screamed inside my head.

"Untie the restraints!"

"You stupid fool."

Praying for freedom was all I could do to take me far, far, away.

CHAPTER THIRTY

FREEDOM CAME FOR me the next day. Two people from the hospital staff came in to my room and released the restraints from my ankle and wrist. I was scheduled to return to work tomorrow, they told me.

As I waited in anticipation for relief to fill my heart, it was absent. I felt nothing. Seeing the restraints dangling from my bedside, I still feared the power they had over me: the hard, leather straps and buckles that kept me in bondage. Even though they were not attached to me, I felt the heaviness of them around my wrists and my ankles. The pressure of the stiff leather dug deeper and deeper into my flesh, even though they were not attached to me; I felt them.

Dressed in the same clothes when I was admitted, I walked out. That doorway was only a few feet away from my bed the entire time. I did not turn to look back at the bed. I kept moving forward, trying to reach the doorway with sluggish steps. Freedom was only a few feet away. While walking, I prayed. Please God, don't let anybody touch me. Please don't let anybody take me prisoner again. Please God, walk beside me and lift me up.

As one foot crossed the doorway, no one grabbed me. My feet began to pick up the pace. The emergency exit door was in view. Pushing the door open, I stumbled down the steps, reached the first floor, and hurried out of the hospital. The medication still had control of my brain, but I kept on walking. Running for my freedom, I never looked back.

CHAPTER THIRTY-ONE

FOUR DAYS IN four-point restraints.

How did I survive through sexual trauma, physically and chemically restrained, the hormone imbalances that lasted for months, and an earthquake and not be an addict roaming the desolate streets today? Or in a mental hospital banging my head up against the wall trying to get rid of the atrocities that never leave my mind? Or possibly dead from the secrets I carried throughout my life until I finally succumbed to their horrors?

I vowed to never speak of the atrocities that happened in those four days. Today, as I write this, I am still afraid they will come and take me away; I never feel safe.

Did anyone witness those crimes and the violation of my basic human rights? Yes, my friends Tim Gunderman and Paula Romes did. Also, people I knew from the Naval Air Support base: Captain Blanca, Captain Blanca's wife, Sue, and my commanding officer at NATO, LCDR K. M. Goldstein. All of them saw me in four point restraints and chemically restrained.

To this day, I still do not know what they kept injecting into my arm. I believe it was Thorazine.

Also, I never saw Lt. Brittain while I was in the restraints, unless he was the vial person that came to my room when darkness fell upon me. Or was it the man who took me to the bathroom and pulled down my underwear?

Not once was I showered, bathed, or given a change of clothes. I laid in my own urine, sweat, blood, and the secretions from the sexual predator who tortured my mind and body.

Tim and Paula visited me while I was restrained. Since my mind was so drugged from all the injections that were pumped into my arm, I don't remember what they said. But I knew that my friends were there. I remembered their faces. Tim told the staff he was my boyfriend to get permission to see me. He told them he was family. Tim knew I wasn't crazy. He knew the capabilities of my mind and witnessed how passive the hospital staff was concerning my situation. However, Tim and Paula never knew about the hormonal disruption or what evilness descended upon me during those four days. No one ever knew. No would ever believe me. The horrors I kept silent. It was the one thing I had control over. I locked them away.

My supervisor LCDR now CDR (commander) K. M. Goldstein was there, but I cannot recall at what time during those four days. I remember her sitting on the right side of my bed. She was horrified and stunned at the very sight of me. I told her not to worry because she had tears in her eyes. I comforted her.

After my release from the hospital, I was promoted to the Staff Message Center in Methods and Results. I stayed in the Navy until August 31, 1984. Then, I was honorably discharged. My evaluation before I left the stated:

"RM3 Turczyn is a faithful and consistent worker who displays tremendous loyalty to her job requirements. She has never hesitated to volunteer her assistance to her supervisor or coworkers and has proven exceptionally valuable in her ability to effectively perform duties in two and sometimes three positions. As a message router, she has the ability to process hundreds of messages within minimum errors. Because of her proficiency at this task, she was picked to work in the Staff Message Center Methods and Results sections. RM3 Turczyn wears the Navy uniform with great pride. Overall 3.8 CDR K. M. Goldstein.

On August 31, 1984, I was released from the Navy with an Honorable Discharge. Underneath my Honorable Discharge were these words, "Other/Physical/Mental Condition – Personality Disorder."

On July 23, 1984 J. L. Brittain wrote in my medical records:

"Mental Status: patient presents as a well-developed female who appears to be her stated age. She is oriented times three and recent remote memory appears to be intact. Speech is clear, soft, and without noticeable defects. Her affect this date was somewhat bizarre and inappropriate and almost schizophrenic in nature. Her mood is depress and despondent. She states that she has had no weight gain or loss. Sensorium appears to be clear and there does not appear to be any illusions, hallucinations, delusions, or other evidence of a thought disorder on mental status exam. Intelligence is estimated to be in the high normal range. Diagnosis: Passive Dependent Personality-Severity of psychosocial stressors, and mild. Highest level of adaptive functioning in the past year: fair. Recommendations: Recommend she be discharged based on a finding of a Personality Disorder, in accordance with NAVMILPERSCOM INST 1910.1. This is severe maladaptive, long standing, and will only continue to cause recurring problems. Prompt administrative separation is suggested. Patient should be continued to be followed in Family Service Center and should be scheduled for at least one weekly visit at Naval Hospital Naples until resolution of the case can be achieved." J.L. Brittain, clinical psychologist.

Personality Disorder is on my DD-214. A DD-214 is comparable to a birth certificate; it shows that it happened during my military service.

This label condemned me as a person and provided an unjust diagnosis. My questions are:

How could I have had that "disorder" and perform as well as I did in the Navy? My evaluations reflected my outstanding behavior and performance.

How could I have ever gotten into the Navy when I passed all of my psychological tests and was granted top-secret clearance?

How could I have been "somewhat bizarre, inappropriate, and almost schizophrenic in nature" when my naval evaluations state differently?

Then, Lt. Brittain states in the same paragraph, "her memory is intact, her sensorium is clear and there are no illusions, hallucinations, delusions, or other evidence of a thought disorder."

And as far as my highest level of adaptability, J. L. Brittain stated, "fair" when I performed beyond the normal expectations in my naval career.

These entire medical and psychiatric atrocities depressed me even more. I wanted to sink into a deep, dark sleep, and never wake up! All my awards and certificates meant nothing!

Up until 1987, I was still experiencing hot flashes, depression, mood swings, and sleep disturbances. I ended up back in the hospital in my hometown due to severe vaginal hemorrhaging.

I had emergency surgery once again. Three times, I was surgically cut in my abdomen area.

My hometown doctor, Dr. Farley, said to my mom and dad, "I

cannot believe she survived. She almost had a bowel obstruction because of all the blood seeping into her peptic cavity."

That little piece of ovary left behind from my second surgery stopped working due to lack of blood flow. Covered in cysts, it ruptured. I believe it stopped working when I was in Naples.

Dr. Farley put me on the hormone replacement therapy drug Premarin for the first time.

I felt alive again, but he took me off Premarin for ten days out of the month. When I was off Premarin, all the symptoms I felt in Italy and for the last three years returned at a rapid pace: depression, mood swings, profuse sweating, insomnia, hot flashes, and crying spells.

Eventually, another doctor examined me from the VA in Iowa City, Iowa.

Keeping me on a daily dosage of estrogen, I felt relief from all my symptoms. One little pill solved everything.

From 1982 until 1987, I went through a menopausal nightmare; a hormonal imbalance.

Feeling normal again, I began to administratively and medically attack the unjust label on my service record and the criminal offenses that took place in Naples, Italy.

For ten years, I tried to get that label removed from my records. I saved all my documentation from the military and the Veterans Administrative Medical Center in Iowa City, Iowa stating that Premarin relieved all my symptoms.

Subjecting myself to three doctors to get the valid medical and psychiatric diagnosis, I went ahead with these rigorous physical and mental examinations.

The doctors I saw were: Dr. Charles De Prosse OB/GYN, Dr. Samuelson, Psychiatry, and Dr. Cromar, General Medicine. They concurred that my symptoms were resolved by taking .625 mg of Premarin, estrogen. A medical and ethical protocol was violated by the unwarranted and criminal use of four point restraints, they agreed.

On September 14, 1990, Dr. Samuelson of Psychiatry stated: "This is a twenty-seven, female from Peru, Illinois. The veteran arranged this evaluation not so much for the purpose of receiving compensation, but because of concern over having been discharged from the Navy on the basis of a psychiatric (personality disorder) diagnosis, the symptoms of which retrospectively seem to have been organic in nature.

The veteran states that during her childhood, she was happy, had friends, was well socialized, and through adolescence did not have any unusual behavior or interpersonal problems. At one point as a teenager, she saw a priest for family problems, but no specifies are listed. She has never threatened suicide, feigned illness, or secondary gain. She was not unusually moody, did not require an unusual amount of reassurance, was not overly dependent for the approval of others, (would not take the role of doormat for others to walk on, and would not necessarily compromise her values to seek approval for others.).

After entering the Navy, she worked as a communications specialist, and stated that she never had any disciplinary problems during her military service. In fact, she received commendations for her participation in NATO exercise overseas. In 1982, she began having gynecological problems. In July 1982, she had removal of uterus, cervix, left fallopian tube and left ovary because of chronic pelvic pain. The pathology revealed an ovarian cyst, which was hemorrhagic and covered with blood clots, swollen, and infiltration with chronic inflammatory cells. Following this surgery, she began having hot flashes, and the onset of a depressed mood, irritability, sleep disturbance (initial and terminal insomnia), feelings of anxiety, occasionally accompanied by tachycardia, and crying spells. These symptoms were very upsetting to the patient, and she carried out her duties in the Navy well. These symptoms gradually worsened and eventually in May of 1984, she nicked her wrist with a razor blade and was hospitalized. Records from this hospitalization were not available, although a report dated July 19, 1984 gave the patient the diagnosis of passive dependent personality, and recommended that she be discharged based on a finding of a personality disorder, in accordance with NAVNILPERSCOMINST 1910.01, May 1983. This is a severe maladaptive, longstanding is not amenable to treatment, and will only continue to cause recurring problems. Prompt administrative separation was suggested by J. L. Brittain.

This **strongly condemning** recommendation was given in spite of the fact that only symptoms of personality disorder listed at the evaluation was her suicidal gesture, the fact that such thoughts of suicide had recurred while she was hospitalized, and the fact that she was having difficulty handing pressures the was experiencing.

For about two and half years following her discharge, she continued to have much difficulty with hot flashes and irritability with waxing and waning, sleep disturbance, and other depressive symptoms, but did not present herself for psychiatric care. Then in 1987, she had a right salpingo-oophorectomy hemorrhagic cyst, thus, taking her only remaining ovary. Thereafter, she was started on estrogen replacement therapy and had a prompt resolution to her hot flashes, irritability, and other depressive symptoms. She was taking replacement therapy on twenty days on and ten days off. During the ten days go off the replacement therapy, she would at times have mild recurrences of depressive symptoms, but not nearly as severe as what she had been experiencing prior to starting replacement therapy. She said that her response to hormone replacement was 'like a miracle drug; for the first time in seven years, I feel normal.'

In 1987, the veteran has had a steady job working as a police force dispatcher, has been social, dating, enjoying her usual activities and denies any thoughts about life not being worth living, any recurrent thoughts about suicide or death wish, and feels like she generally has a new lease on life.

Other than the medical problems referred to above, she has had no other prominent medical problems.

Mental Status Exam: Casually dressed, well-kept, good eye contact, normal psychomotor activity, mood neutral. Affect was full and appropriate. Mental content was without suicidal ideation or psychotic features. The veteran was cooperative with the interview, and no time made any statements that were manipulative, aggressive, or seemed overly dramatic. Her attire was appropriate. Intellect was alert and fully oriented. Insight and judgment intact.

History of Organic Affective Disorder, in remission. Hormone Replacement Therapy.

From this interview with the patient and review of her file, there is **no** indication of her history or her presentation of a personality disorder. Given the temporal relationship symptoms were of an organic nature and such represented an organic affective disorder which began while in the military." Stephen Samuelson, M.D. Psychiatry.

The results determined that I never had a personality disorder, but my symptoms resulted from premature menopause after having had certain creative organs surgically removed.

Elated to have the truth revealed, I presented all my medical and psychiatric records, military evaluations, awards, and certificates to the Naval Board of Corrections in Washington, D.C., to get the personality disorder label removed from my DD-214.

The Naval Board ruled against the VA doctors and stated,

"A three-member panel of the Board of Naval Records, sitting in executive session, considered your application on 3 October 1991. Your allegations of errors and injustices were reviewed in accordance with administrative regulations and procedures applicable to the proceedings of the board. After careful and conscientious consideration of the entire record, the board found that the evidence submitted was insufficient to establish the existence of probable material errors or injustices. Accordingly, your application has been denied. The names of the members of the panel will be furnished upon request." W. Dean Pfeiffer, Executive Director.

And of course, I asked for their names. They were Mr. George N. Brezna, Mr. Frederick P. Anthony, and Ms. Rossie S. Payne. Three people had decided my fate for the rest of my life.

However, there was strong documentation in my favor from the Chairman, Department of Psychiatry, and a Special Advisor for Psychiatry on the Naval Board of Corrections. The report stated:

"Review of the BCNR (Board for Corrections of Naval Records) notes that former RM3 Turczyn is requesting that her reason for separation 'other physical/mental condition-personality disorder' be changed to a medical discharge based on the information noted above. The personality disorder diagnosis was not substantiated by information included in the records. Her allegations of a misdiagnosis would appear to be substantiated by this retrospective review of the records. I recommend that former RM3 Turczyn's request be approved." K.S. Hoyle, CDR, MC, USN Acting Chairman 16 May 1990.

Unfortunately, the board did not listen to the Department of Psychiatry Special Advisor for Psychiatry findings. The board remained firm in its decision. Another grave injustice took place in my life I could not understand. What happened to the truth?

The emotional journey to correct my DD-214 killed my spirit. I could not believe the blatant lies and deceit. I resubmitted my file for further evaluation again. However, the board denied my claim once again.

From November 1, 2001 to June 30, 2007, over 26,000 enlisted military personnel were discharged with the diagnosis of personality disorder. The Government Accountability Office studied the files. A vast majority of these service men and women were deployed overseas and/or victims of military sexual trauma. A personality disorder is considered a pre-existing condition. So how did 26,000 men and women pass their psychological tests? I believe that these men and women have PTSD. However, if they are discharged under *personality disorder*, the government is not responsible to pay for their disability benefits because this diagnosis is considered to be a pre-existing condition.

The courageous women and men of this country defend our freedoms, constitution, and country. Veterans should not be subjected to any unnecessary administrative battlefields in order to receive their benefits that they so rightly deserve.

CHAPTER THIRTY-TWO

THE AFTERMATH WAS just as destructive as their heinous crimes. Feelings of anger, regret, guilt, shame, remorse, and most all depression hovered over me like a rain cloud. But I just kept on running and moving. I never looked back. Unfortunately, the traumas started to take on lives of their own. Fear was my driving factor in the front seat of my life. It ruled me for forty-five years. At times, fear took a hold of my hand and convinced me that staying silent was the course to follow. It crushed my voice to scream out to the world about the horrors that kept me in bondage and to expose those barbaric crimes.

The physical and verbal abuse continued throughout my life. But this time, it wasn't my father who beat me with his belt or hands. It was men: military personnel, boyfriends, and husbands. They beat and choked me with their fists, held me under water, kicked my knees until they were the size of cantaloupes, and dragged me down concrete porch steps. Feeling each step pound into my soft flesh, I was smashed onto the sidewalk like broken glass. I have nursed so many black eyes with cold compresses, I have lost count. And of course, there were bruises that never seemed to fade away.

A life filled with shame. This was my life.

In my twenties, I went from one abusive marriage to another. Abusive relationships continued until I entered my forties. Then, I married one more time, which made it number three, but it didn't last either. Though this was not an abusive marriage, we were two people needing different things in life.

I would have done anything for someone to love me. Abusive behavior was part of my pathetic world because I allowed it. One cannot exist without self-worth and love.

I have seen trauma victims self-medicate, drink alcohol, take illegal and abused prescription drugs, shop until financially ruined, and gamble until they lost everything in order to stop the pain.

My coping behavior was cutting.

Self-injury-cutting typically is not a suicide attempt. It's an unhealthy coping technique used to deal with emotional pain, frustration, and anger. Self-injury is an impulsive behavior problem linked to women and men who have been raped, sexually molested, sodomized, tortured, and includes other mental health issues, such as depression.

The targets of this behavior are the torso, arms, and legs. One of the many scars I carry today is on my right arm, which needed eighteen stitches inside and seventeen stitches on the outside.

Whenever I cut, an immediate sense of relief came over me, while watching the blood stream down my arm, depending upon how deep the cut was that day. Euphoria and calmness come over me as the stress dripped away from my body along with the blood. Sadly, I felt deserving of the pain. Then, the guilt and shame followed with the return of the emotional pain. It was a vicious cycle.

And, there was one suicide attempt in 1996.

The crimes that took place in Italy, were buried and blocked so deep inside my brain, they were trying to burst out when I began to feel better from the hormone replacement therapy. These feelings came out like monsters.

I began cutting, drinking, moving from state to state, always trying to keep one step ahead of the pain and to keep the horrors locked away. Never getting close to anyone, or the people I did were unhealthy like me, even with friends and most all, family. I could never sit still long enough to allow myself to feel and recover. Nurturing my pain wasn't a therapeutic strategy I utilized. I had not discovered the path of recovery, yet. Plus, going to a counselor or a psychiatrist frightened me even more. What if the psychologist unlawfully chemically and physically restrained me again?

Angry, I broke furniture, smashed mirrors, and banged my head and fists against walls. Cutting became my way to deal with these monsters.

Also, I become a work alcoholic. I graduated from Illinois Valley Community College (Dean's list) and made the National Honors List after completing one semester at Texas Woman's University. I received my undergraduate degree from Northern Illinois University.

I have held many jobs, prestigious positions, but moved away when the pain began to surface. Always running - never stopping for a moment.

Ironically, I gravitated towards the stress. The more I had in my life, the deeper the feelings stayed buried. If I worked harder, got more awards and raises, I could prove my worth to my family and myself.

See, look at me, I am working for the government again at the Department of Veterans Affairs as a Veterans Service Representative, as a Child Protective Service Agent, teaching at a community college, and the Humane Education Manager at the SPCA. I am appearing on radio shows, appearing on Fox 4 Live featuring *Dog of the Day*, speaking on behalf of Disabled American Veterans, and a writer for the Veterans' News and Views.

Labels and titles mean nothing. Loving and self-care mean everything.

Living a fallacy, I believed that my positions in the work environment along with the labels and titles identified my value. I followed a path to self-destruction.

Who was this woman with no name?

Before happiness, freedom, and love could enter my life, I had to save myself, acknowledge the traumas, conquer the atrocities that had occurred throughout my life, and most importantly, unlock the room of fear and denial. Opening the door of that room terrified me.

CHAPTER THIRTY-THREE

RECOVERY IS A process and an intense journey. For me, it was more of a discovery; a slow unraveling of emotional layers. Educating myself about human behavior and the cognitive development process of the brain empowered me.

I had to answer the following questions: Why was I always moving, running, living in fear, allowing people to abuse me, and communicating in anger when triggered. What were my triggers? How can I protect myself, learn to use balance in my life, and why was I cutting?

College was the beginning of the recovery process. While living in Las Vegas, the educational arena became my support system. Most of all, the teachers became my mentors.

Just like boot camp, military school, and on my navy evaluations, I received positive feedback. The college professors introduced me to writing, literature, history, and literary authors who inspired and taught me about making life choices. These women stood up for themselves, experienced pain, love, friendship, prejudices, and freedom.

The following instructors: Rose Hawkins, Dr. Diane Swanson, Dr. Winston, Stephen Rhoades, Dr. Clifton, and Dr. Barbara Presnall, introduced me to Anne Sexton, Sylvia Plath, John Milton, Shakespeare, Charlotte Perkins Gilman, Robert Frost, Emily Dickinson, Flannery O'Connor, Maya Angelou, Alice Walker, Julian of Norwich, Martin Luther King Jr., Elizabeth Barrett Browning, and my beloved Bronte sisters: Charlotte, Emily, and Anne. These authors expressed the way I felt inside. With their words, they encouraged me to continue on with my journey in recovery. They empowered me. I could always run to them for help by reading and rereading their works. Finding solace and guidance in books opened up the raw emotions and allowed me to feel. We were kindred spirits because they wrote about my pain, the losses, the deepest regrets, and failures. They instilled hope inside of my wounded soul. The journey of self-love had finally begun.

While attending college in Las Vegas, I went to a VA clinic and said to one of the nurse practitioners, "I think I have this thing called PTSD (Post-Traumatic Stress Disorder)."

As usual, it was overlooked, but my mental health progress notes stated, "Veteran has symptoms of PTSD."

The year was 1991. So, I started to do my own research on mental health. Realizing I had to get some help, I saw a counselor named Mary.

Although I stayed in Las Vegas for only a few years before moving again, Mary began to help me peel away those layers of pain. Allowing one layer to be removed at a time, I began therapy.

PTSD is an emotional and a psychological reaction to trauma - a painful and shocking experience. It can have lasting effects for survivors. They feel that their lives have changed completely.

Some of the symptoms include nightmares, flashbacks, and anxiety. The physical symptoms include: headaches, nausea, stomach pain, and heart palpitations. Also, insomnia, jumpiness, irritability, outbursts of anger, isolation, hyper vigilance, memory issues, and difficulty concentrating occurs.

I have irritable bowel syndrome, anxiety disorder, a bladder condition, heart palpations, anxiety attacks, flashbacks, insomnia, hyper vigilance, a tendency to isolate and avoid, persistent depression disorder (related to PTSD), self-injury (related to PTSD), and more.

My triggers are noises, certain smells, authoritative figures, crowds, the night, heat, driving, and enclosed spaces and more. I used to sleep with a large knife under my bed for years, in case I had to free myself.

I live a structured life. My house is organized, I work out on a daily basis, do not allow a lot of busyness in one day, and practice balance in my life.

When I go to the grocery store and the movies, it is early in the morning to avoid the crowds. I cannot drive at night anymore. Plus, there are many other strategies I have learned over the years about how to deal with my daily life. Sometimes, it is so exhausting to plan everything out to the avoid triggers especially when I travel, I have to cancel all my plans and rest my mind.

My brain will never be the same again. These symptoms are just not psychological. As a result of traumas, the hippocampus, the part of my brain that is involved in learning, storing, retrieving explicit memories, and handling stress, has experienced a physical change. The hippocampus works closely with the prefrontal cortex that regulates my emotional responses to fear and stress. The amygdala is the most notably altered part of my brain affected with PTSD, and it too, works closely with the hippocampus.

The amygdala decodes emotions, especially stimuli that threaten me. Any signs of danger or fear are sent to the amygdala, which gets it fired up to start sending out a "fight" or "flight" signal. My brain has reduced activity in the ventromedial prefrontal cortex (vmPFC), the more sophisticated part of the brain that processes emotions and is involved in decision making. I have increased activity in my amygdala. Therefore, the door to my amygdala will never close. It will always be open to producing more intense anxiety symptoms, the key features in PTSD. In other words, my prefrontal cortex does not communicate with my amygdala. The amygdala door is like a flap. This was how my psychologist explained it to me. The door will always be open to send out more enzymes to keep the fearful responses unmonitored.

Basically, some people are put on anti-depressants to help "shut" the amygdala door slightly, and to help with their anxiety. Taking anti-depressants worked for me during a certain period in my life. But now, I cannot tolerate them.

When I hear people say, "You know she has PTSD," it saddens me. I never asked for these debilitating physical, psychological, and medical conditions.

Just like our veterans did not ask to have their arms, legs, or minds sacrificed to the tragedy of war.

Another form of support entered my life just like my college professors, the Veterans Administration Mental Health counselors, and psychologists. Believe me, because of the stigma that follows, I was scared to step foot in the hallway of a mental health facility.

Taking care of my mental health is just as important as taking care of my medical health. Mental health dictates medical health.

Richard Keil, Dr. Jule Moravec, and Dr. Amy Wrabetz were my mental health providers at the VA. They showed me support, care, and guidance. Most importantly, they believed me.

Mr. Keil was the first social worker that helped me to express my feelings of shame while I was in Illinois. But, I never let him in or told him anything that would be therapeutic to my recovery. It was a start.

When I moved to Arizona, Dr. Moravec was my mental health care provider. For the first time, a doctor correctly diagnosed me with PTSD. One year later after meeting with Dr. Moravec, I stopped talking about everyone else and focused on my problems. My true journey to recovery started in 2003.

After a twenty-two year administrative and medical battle with the Veterans Administration for compensation due to service connected disabilities, (disabilities that occurred while on active duty), I was finally granted my service connected disability for PTSD in 2006.

I was validated and vindicated that I did not have a personality disorder. Even though the Board of Naval Corrections did not take responsibility for the crimes that took place in Italy, the Veterans Administration diagnosed me properly after years of documentation I continued to submit.

Since 2008, I have been seeing Dr. Amy Wrabetz, the program manager of the mental health department at the Northern Arizona Veterans Administration Healthcare System in Prescott, Arizona. When I think or write about Dr. Wrabetz, tears filled with gratitude stream down my face. What she has done for me would take years to tell you.

Many times, I came to her office sheltering my face inside the loneliness of my arms, too weary to speak of the shame and horrors. Patiently, she waited for me to release the emotional bondage that kept me imprisoned for so many years. She has been by my side through relapses and the healing process. Dr. Wrabetz nurtured my dying heart and helped it grow into a fresh heart full of self-love, self-respect, honor, dignity, and value. But I, too, did the hard work. She is my hero.

I was ready for a change in my life and to tackle all the intense work and to step on that emotional battlefield. I rose to face those monsters filled with evil spirits. With my sword of valor, I slayed shame, fear, self-doubt, guilt, low self-esteem, anger, self-hatred, and abuse. Warriors of love, joy, patience, peace, happiness, and forgiveness joined me, as I began to rule in my new world.

Today, I am fifty-one years old. I am reaching new plateaus and continually learning during my journey in recovery. Learning to respect my PTSD and to keep a balance in life have been difficult hurdles for me to overcome.

My people pleasing days are over. However, in recovery, there are setbacks-relapses. I have survived many unexpected challenges on this journey in recovery: the loss of my mother and homelessness.

In 1998, I was thirty-five when I lost my mother to stomach cancer.

As she came closer to death, we became closer as mother and daughter. I cared for her every need and made her as comfortable as possible. We sat in the bathtub together, my mother in front of me and I clothed in a T-shirt and gym shorts, while I bathed her twice a day to keep her dignity. Sitting behind her with the washrag in my hand, I looked at the bruises all over her back that surfaced through her translucent skin. The cancer was pushing out her internal organs. Her stomach was as swollen as a woman in her eighth month of pregnancy. Cancer was killing her quickly. Ma and I would take our afternoon naps in the comforter that I still wrap around myself every night. She told me how afraid she was to die.

I told her not to worry because God will be right there waiting for her with open arms as Jesus leads the way. Heaven is our final resting place, and this is just a quick stop. The earth.

Ma wished she had my faith. It bothered her that she couldn't pray or concentrate any more.

"I'm praying for you," I said.

My mother asked me to write her eulogy, and I did.

One week before my mother died, she said, "One day, you will become a great writer."

I just wanted my mom to be proud of me.

She never got to see me walk across the stage when I graduated from Northern Illinois University. But what mattered the most to me was the time we spent together healing wounds from the past through conversations, hand holding, and laughter. We became the mother and daughter I had always hoped we would be.

While lying in her hospital bed, ma asked me, dad, and Janie to hold hands.

"You must stick together after I am gone," she said.

We held hands and promised to stay together.

Unfortunately, we did not obey her wishes.

My sister and father remained close, but I am estranged from the family. Understanding PTSD is difficult because it is an invisible disability. Education and support are the key factors in helping family members with this condition.

It would break my mother's heart to know that we are not a family any more.

Surrendering and forgiveness have welcomed me.

The last time my father came close striking me again was one week after mom passed away. I was thirty-five years old. Me, Janie, Dawn (a social worker from Illinois Valley Community Hospital), and my father were sitting at the kitchen table. I shut down completely and basically stopped communicating. Janie and my father kept saying to Dawn that I was not speaking to them.

I had nothing to say. Dealing with my grief and loss, I wondered about what I should do now. I just buried my mother and was in a constant fog. Inches before my body, my father slammed his fist on the table like a hammer because he demanded that I speak. I stood up and ran out of the house. A hug-all I wanted was a hug after I watched my mother die. He never even hugged me.

At thirty-nine, I became homeless with my three dogs: Alex, Bronte, and Cosette. We stayed on a floor in Phoenix, in my car, and then in the Bradshaw Mountains. I pray to God every day that I never have to be in that situation again. Frankly, I have not healed from that area in my life, yet. When I speak about sleeping on the floor in a person's living room with three dogs guarding me, or bathing in a McDonald's restroom, I am riddled with anxiety. To this day, my car is sacred to me because it provides shelter. The shame of sending emails to over fifty family members asking them for five dollars and not one person responding, showed me humility. Tossing aside any morals that I possessed in order to have shelter for my dogs and me, sickens me to this day. Twice, I was homeless. It is a dark hole filled with debilitating depression, suffering, and humiliation. I cannot fathom going back there.

I have learned a lot of life lessons as my journey continues.

*I have learned that fear has kept me from living my life and loving myself.

*I have learned that stuffing emotional issues will eventually kill your spirit.

*I have learned that my whole life has been filled with unhealthy relationships on all levels. I sacrificed my morals, values, integrity, safety, and dreams, hoping to get anybody to love me. I have given up money, feelings, and thoughts to please other people who did not have my best interest at heart.

*I have learned that I have harmful behaviors from PTSD.

I denied the pain of my past. So instead, I sought relief from self-mutilating, eating sugary foods, and trying to help other people, so I didn't have to deal with the traumas.

*Every time I plunged a razor blade or a piece of glass into my wrists, legs, or chest, I felt that I deserved to be punished. I do not deserve to be maltreated by anybody, including myself.

*I have learned to allow myself to feel the pain of not being able to have children.

*I have learned that keeping busy stopped me from dealing with my emotions.

*I have learned to respect my PTSD.

*I have learned that I am seeking the truth about myself.

*I have learned that I am a strong-willed woman who is a Warrior.

*I have learned that I am responsible for my actions and behaviors no matter what happened in my past.

*I have learned that instinct is my internal compass and to always listen to it because it has never pointed me in the wrong direction. Every time I ignored my instinct and let EGO drive, it turned out to be a devastating detour.

*Most of all, I have learned to surrender and to forgive myself.

Also, I have learned that I would die and kill for my country. I have always asked myself these questions: Can you, Debra Jean, take another life if your country and your own life is threatened? When I held up my right hand and stated, *I will support and defend the Constitution of the United States against all enemies, foreign and domestic*, was I just going through a formality?

Until you are put in a war zone or a situation like I was in 1984, rendering you to use your training to save your own life or members of the military that is threatened by foreign forces with intentions to cause bodily or deadly harm, only then, can you answer that question. Mine was answered in Naples, Italy.

Remember Squeeze Alley? I am glad I listened to Brownie that day about how to strategically move in and out of that narrow street because it saved my life.

Ronald Regan proposed the Strategic Defense Initiative on March 23, 1983. Demonstrations overseas near the military bases had commenced.

I was driving into Squeeze Alley for my 7:00 pm to 7:00 am shift at the NATO base when I came to a dead stop before reaching the bottle neck. All of a sudden, I was free to move forward with my Volkswagen bug. Immediately, my instincts told me not to go through the alley, but I didn't want to be late for work. As soon as my Volkswagen, with the AFI (American Forces Italy) license plate (a dead giveaway that I was an American), reached the middle of Squeeze Alley, I saw the walls of fire bellowing towards the sky.

The Italians were protesting against President Regan for bringing nuclear warheads into Sicily. Knowing that the Americans took Squeeze Alley into the NATO and the Naval Air Station bases, they closed off three streets with walls of fire. Tractor tires sat across the entrance ways to the streets. They set the massive tires ablaze with kerosene.

Dead center in the intersection, I was surrounded by walls of fire. Squeeze Alley was behind me.

We were rats trapped rats lured into fire. I was the leader of the pack. There were many others that were behind me. As I sat in fear for my life, a boy about twelve years old came up to my opened window. With a Molotov cocktail in his hand, he screamed at me. Inches from my face, I saw the dirty rag hanging from the glass bottle. Inside, the deadly liquid waited to implode as he lit the dangling rag. Another young person tried to break my windshield with a small tire. As he threw it at my windshield, it bounced back, but cracked it into a spider's web. A few of the glass pieces landed in my face.

Adrenaline flowed like lava through my veins. I put my Volkswagen in gear and went right for the wall of fire in front of me. As soon as I was about to go through the wall, I turned the steering wheel to the left. My car squealed around to face Squeeze Alley. Flooring the gas pedal, I rammed the stick shift. I turned into a person I never knew existed; I was completely in control of saving my life.

Vehicles came at me, as I drove the car onto the sidewalk. Protestors ran as they tried to get out of the way. I didn't care what I hit or ran over. I was getting the hell out of there. I made it through with cuts on my face. Surprisingly, I was alive. At that moment, that realization that I was going to die and that Molotov cocktail was inches from my face, answered the questions. I can still smell the fire and kerosene and see the hatred for Americans plastered over that young boy's face.

***

Yes, I still believe in God and my faith. I believe God is love.

I believe dogs are love. The universe is filled with love and unknown angels who have helped me on my journey. Unknown because they do not seek attention or ask for favors in return. Angels because they are truly God messengers here on earth. They clothe themselves with compassion, gentleness, and thoughtfulness. Through our trials and tribulations, they walk among us. These unknown angels stood by me when my eyes grew wide with fear, and my heart was filled with an aching sorrow.

Ironically though, if you asked people who knew me throughout my fifty-one years they would say, "She is so motivated. She is so driven. There goes Debra Jean the Jelly Bean!"

My journey continues, as I walk upon the earth's arena carefully nurturing the new heart that beats inside this body. I will never forget the journey that carried me here. The scars on my body remind me of the thorns on a rose bush. They were meant to teach me to parent myself, to walk side by side with faith, and to never lose myself for the selfish benefit of another.

And had it not been for the grace of my Lord and Savior, I would not be here today.

I was *A Woman with No Name.*

I was the nameless person standing in the back of the church during Sunday morning services. I was the student sitting in an English literature classroom. I was the nameless face with the black, purple, blue, and green bruises, as I walked into the Safe House. I was a body that carried my sole possessions packed in a blanket of frayed woven dreams. I was the woman who walked with bloody footprints from days of traveling through storms of suffering, searching for my identity.

***

Shuffling the streets in the morning shade
She inspects the delicacies of waste choosing her slighted menu
Dancing felines linger on top of tins patiently waiting for human reach to retrieve spoiled survival
The loaf of mold tucked close to her heart, a paper domain, no table to dine
Diplomacies in life tacked to cardboard walls
A photo of a child nestled to her breast
Did the years deteriorate along with forged dreams?
Or has it been only yesterday that I wore your wedding ring?
Watercolor paintings of people tacked to the cardboard walls, though hollow are their eyes
Can't society see the destruction of men left behind?
She was your daughter
A sister and your best friend
A lady in love
She is a Woman with No Name

***

As my journey and recovery continues, I am learning to live a new life filled with peace and love. Remaining in the present has given me joy. I stand at the core essence of reinventing myself just like I have been given a new body, soul, and heart: a fresh journey. At times, I still feel a little bit shaky and unsure of myself, but that's ok. I ponder about going back to Naples, Italy and walking into that room without fear and hesitation and leaving it all behind like ashes in the wind. But for now, I am taking this precious gift of a new life and embracing it. Because I know that today, I am free. I am finally, free.

***

I am a Woman with a Name, and my name is Debra Jean.

Free

I stand upon this mountain of knowledge
The wind's wrath conceals my nakedness
My head tilts towards heaven as the sun pours its shine into my dark soul
An awakening of dormant emotions rise to the surface of my perished skin
Released from bondage as the chains from the past crumble around my feet
Starving eyes, starving arms, reaching
Love come to me
I am ready to fly
I have finally been set free

ABOUT THE AUTHOR

Debra Jean spends her time in the American southwest writing her next novel and practicing a healthy life style. She enjoys hiking, traveling, cooking, reading, traveling, and sharing her journeys.

Made in the USA
Charleston, SC
27 August 2015